NEED TO GET YOUR
WRITING CAREER MOVING?

FIND OUT HOW AT LONDON BOOK FAIR – THE WORLD'S LEADING SPRING BOOK FAIR

The Daily Mail and English PEN Masterclasses:

● How to Get Published   ● Contemporary Fiction
● Poetry   ● Historical Fiction

All led by leading authors who will guide
you towards a fulfilling writing career.

Classes will run 12–13 March.
Visit: **www.lbf-masterclasses.co.uk/granta**

LitIdol is once again searching for the next
international bestseller! This year the renowned
competition will focus on 'Crime/Thriller' writing.

Win representation from top literary agency
Curtis Brown.

For more details visit: **www.litidol.co.uk/granta**

13–15 March 2005   London Olympia, UK   www.lbf-virtual.com

GRANTA 88, WINTER 2004
www.granta.com

EDITOR *Ian Jack*
DEPUTY EDITOR *Matt Weiland*
MANAGING EDITOR *Fatema Ahmed*
ASSOCIATE EDITOR *Liz Jobey*
EDITORIAL ASSISTANT *Helen Gordon*

CONTRIBUTING EDITORS *Diana Athill, Sophie Harrison, Gail Lynch, Blake Morrison, John Ryle, Sukhdev Sandhu, Lucretia Stewart*

ASSOCIATE PUBLISHER *Sally Lewis*
FINANCE *Geoffrey Gordon, Morgan Graver*
SALES *Frances Hollingdale*
PUBLICITY *Louise Campbell*
SUBSCRIPTIONS *John Kirkby, Julie Walker*
PUBLISHING ASSISTANT *Mark Williams*
ADVERTISING MANAGER *Kate Rochester*
PRODUCTION ASSOCIATE *Sarah Wasley*
PROOFS *Gillian Kemp*

PUBLISHER *Rea S. Hederman*

Granta, 2–3 Hanover Yard, Noel Road, London N1 8BE
Tel 020 7704 9776 Fax 020 7704 0474
email for editorial: editorial@granta.com

Granta US, 1755 Broadway, 5th Floor, New York, NY 10019-3780, USA

TO SUBSCRIBE call 020 7704 0470 or e-mail subs@granta.com
A one-year subscription (four issues) costs £26.95 (UK), £34.95 (rest of Europe) and £41.95 (rest of the world).

Granta is printed and bound in Italy by Legoprint. The paper used in this publication meets the minimum requirements of American National Standard for Information Sciences—Permanence of Paper for Printed Library Materials, ANSI Z39.48-1984.

Granta is published by Granta Publications.
This selection copyright © 2004 Granta Publications.

Design: Slab Media.
Front cover photograph: Istock

ISBN 0-903141-73-6

Hanif Kureishi

My Ear At His Heart

The most extraordinary memoir of the year from the
bestselling author of The Buddha of Suburbia and Intimacy

A moving journey from Bombay to suburbia following
the birth of a writer and the father he came to understand

Available from all good bookshops and from www.faber.co.uk

ff

MOTHERS

GRANTA

david sedaris

Dress Your Family in Corduroy and Denim

'This is a man who could capture your heart
and lift your spirits while reading out the
ingredients of a rice cake' *Observer*

'If you haven't come across David Sedaris,
get in quick before over-exposure
sucks him dry' *Guardian*

Radio 4's
Book of the Week,
from 10 January 2005

ABACUS
Imprint of the Year

Also available in

Time Warner
AudioBooks

Motley Notes

The last issue of *Granta* celebrated its twenty-fifth anniversary and retraced a little of its pre-1979 history as a magazine for and by the students of Cambridge University. Soon after it was published, I got a letter from prisoner number FF8782 at Her Majesty's Prison in Maidstone, Kent.

Dear Ian Jack,
I seem to remember that whilst I was up at Cambridge in the late 60s I edited a special edition of GRANTA, along with my friend SCOTT WALKER (of The Walker Brothers).
Have you come across a copy of that issue? I wonder if you have any spare copies on file.
In the light of recent interesting events, I thought it might be a curious and interesting addition to your celebrations!
Life continues to be fascinating. I'm up for parole next March, having by then served three and a half years for crimes I didn't commit.
What an enjoyably varied existence I've been lucky enough to lead. As an observer of the human condition, I've seen it all (well, nearly all).
Best wishes,
Jonathan

The writer was Jonathan King, former record producer, musical arranger and, long ago and briefly, pop star ('Everyone's Gone to the Moon'). In November 2001, King was given a seven-year prison sentence on one count of buggery, one of attempted buggery, and four of indecent assault against five men who at the time of the offences were all under the age of sixteen. The dates of the offences ranged from 1981 to 1987. That, it seemed to me, was one of the problems with the case: why had these men waited up to twenty years to come forward with their complaints? Another problem with it was the cooperation of the victims in the crimes against them. Of the five men who testified against King, four visited his home willingly and frequently to be assaulted. All were fifteen or fourteen years of age. They had often been picked up by King in his Rolls-Royce and driven to his flat. There they had enjoyed good food and drink and a kind of friendship. One man said in court: 'My father thought he was good and my family thought it was exciting. I was flattered at being friends with him but I had a big secret which I could not tell anyone about.' A big secret is a burdensome thing, no doubt, even if it is to others no more than the common experience of adolescent boys in a boarding-school dormitory. The burden was lightened, however, when at the end of the trial one or two of the victims sold their secrets to newspapers and shared them with millions of readers using nouns such as 'ordeal' and 'torment'.

Still, the law is the law. People over the age of sixteen should not be having sex with people under that age, even if the common perception of fourteen and fifteen year olds now is that they are all at each other like knives. And when does a pederast become a paedophile? At the time of King's trial, England's popular hatred of paedophiles as abusers and corrupters (and sometimes killers) of children had reached new heights and this may have influenced police interest in King. Perhaps the distinction between the two words can never be drawn: if, aged forty, you fancy a boy of fifteen, who's to say that your tastes might not range down to a ten year old? Therefore you might argue that King certainly deserved to go to jail, though what good it did anyone is hard to see. But seven years? In the Victorian year of 1895, for similar offences, Oscar Wilde got only two, and now there is a little statue of him just off Trafalgar Square. A final concern about the case is what the judge is reported to have said at King's sentencing: 'It may well be that your time in prison will not be easy,' a statement from which it is hard not to infer: 'You are, in prison parlance, a nonce, and nonces ain't popular with their fellow prisoners, so watch out, my little gay friend.'

Late in 2001 I wrote a piece for the *Guardian* which mentioned some of these facts and arguments, and King got in touch from prison, submitting an article which we politely declined. I have never met him, which may be just as well; his gift for relentless self-promotion is legendary. Nor can we find an issue of *Granta* which was edited by him and Scott Walker, though that's not to say it never existed. I hope it did and, in somebody's attic, still does. The Walker Brothers had spectacular hits in the late Sixties with 'Make It Easy on Yourself' and 'The Sun Ain't Gonna Shine Anymore'. I remember the songs—who doesn't?—though I sometimes confuse the singers with The Righteous Brothers of the same period. The three Walkers were American, but moved to Britain in 1965. Scott Walker was born Scott Engel in Ohio. As Richie Unterberger writes in the web's All Music Guide: 'They weren't named Walker, they weren't brothers, and they weren't English, but they nevertheless became part of the British Invasion [of American popular music].'

Scott later went solo. According to Unterberger, he was inspired by the lyrics of Jacques Brel and wrote songs about 'oddball subjects— prostitutes, transvestites, suicidal brooders, plagues, and Joseph Stalin'. In turn, he was 'a substantial, if largely overlooked' influence on the singing style of David Bowie and Bryan Ferry. Today, he is 'a notoriously reclusive figure, who has rarely been interviewed or even seen in public since his days of stardom'.

Some of these traits of character and taste suggest he might have been well-suited to edit *Granta*: The Suicidal Brooders Issue!—with or without Jonathan King. We know precisely where inmate FF8782 resides—in County Road, Maidstone, Kent, beneath that little tent of blue which prisoners call the sky. But where is Scott Walker? At *Granta*, if only to help unravel an archival mystery, it would be good to know.

Nuha al-Radi died on August 31, 2004, aged sixty-three. She was a painter and sculptor and also an occasional and very good diarist of events in Baghdad. She died of leukaemia, which she believed had been caused by the many tons of depleted uranium that America and its allies had fired at Iraqi tanks during the 1991 war. She was an Iraqi, though no friend of the Ba'athist regime which her parents fled in 1969. A lot of her life was spent shuttling between London, New York and Beirut, which she quit for Baghdad after civil war broke out in Lebanon in 1975. Beirut eventually became her home again—she is buried there—but Baghdad and her friends and family who lived in the city were visitable and never far from her mind.

Her diaries of the first Iraq war were first published in *Granta* in 1992—they became a book six years later. In 2003, we published her diary of the second Iraq war. Being a good and interesting diarist, as anyone who has tried to keep a diary will know, is harder than it looks. The temptation to make one important to one's self is usually present, and when one is bang in the middle of the world's biggest story there is the additional temptation of researching and writing like a reporter and having Big Thoughts. The beauty of Nuha's diaries lay in their quickness and simplicity and complete lack of writerly self-consciousness. They revealed the persistence of ordinary life, as most of us know it (visiting aunties, making cakes, gardening), against an awful background of violence, fear and hardship. The entry for May 13, 2003 reads: 'Tonight there is a big halo round the moon. Rumsfeld has declared that their presence in Iraq is an occupation, finally. Who were they kidding anyway?'

Two weeks later she records a joke that was current in the city during the American bombing. Several of Saddam's famous body doubles have been summoned to a meeting. They are told that there is good news and bad news. 'Saddam's still alive, that's the good news. The bad news is that he lost both his arms and legs…'

With certain brilliant exceptions—the English novelist Margaret Forster has written one of them—it is fathers rather than mothers who until recently have hogged the limelight in family memoirs. Think of the books of Edmund Gosse, V. S. Pritchett, Blake Morrison, or the smaller accounts of Raymond Carver or Angela Carter. It is hard to know exactly why, but part of the explanation may be that, once upon a time, fathers and not mothers were the parents who went out to work, whose presence and temper were less certain, whose love (to a child) seemed more conditional, whose careers offered a more linear narrative, whose lives were more superficially dramatic. And, being men, they were also the parents who on average died earlier, making it possible for them to be written about sooner—by their material-hunting, ruthless children.

This issue of *Granta* rights a little of the imbalance. It's mainly about the individuality of mothers and motherhood. No more need be said.

Ian Jack

GRANTA

THE LANES
John McGahern

John McGahern (second from the right in the back row) with
his father, sisters and young brother.

The Lanes

The soil in Leitrim is poor, in places no more than an inch deep. Underneath is either daub, a blue-grey modelling clay, or channel, a compacted gravel. Neither can absorb the heavy rainfall. Rich crops of rushes and wiry grasses keep the thin clay from being washed away.

These fields between the lakes are small, separated by thick hedges of whitethorn, ash, blackthorn, alder, sally, rowan, wild cherry, green oak, sycamore, and the lanes that link them under the low mountains are narrow, often with high banks. The hedges are the glory of these small fields, especially when the hawthorn foams into streams of blossom each May and June. The sally is the first tree to green and the first to wither, and the rowan berries are an astonishing orange in the light from the lakes every September. These hedges are full of mice and insects and small birds, and sparrowhawks can be seen hunting all through the day. In their branches the wild woodbine and dog rose give off a deep fragrance in summer evenings, and on their banks grow the foxglove, the wild strawberry, primrose and fern and vetch among the crawling briars. The beaten pass the otter takes between the lakes can be traced along these banks and hedges, and in quiet places on the edge of the lakes are the little lawns speckled with fish bones and blue crayfish shells where the otter feeds and trains her young. Among the rushes and wiry grasses also grow the wild orchid and the windflower. The very poorness of the soil saved these fields when old hedges and great trees were being levelled throughout Europe for factory farming, and, amazingly, amid unrelenting change, these fields have hardly changed at all since I ran and played and worked in them as a boy. Among the rushy hills and small lakes, surprising islands of rich green limestone are also to be found.

A maze of lanes links the houses that are scattered sparsely about these fields, and the lanes wander into one another like streams until they reach some main road. These narrow lanes are still in use. In places, the hedges that grow on the high banks along the lanes are so wild that the trees join and tangle above them to form a roof, and in the full leaf of summer it is like walking through a green tunnel pierced by vivid pinpoints of light.

I came back to live among these lanes thirty years ago. My wife and I were beginning our life together, and we thought we could make a bare living on these small fields and I would write. It was a time when we could have settled almost anywhere, and if she had not liked the place and the people we would have moved elsewhere. I, too, liked the place, but I was from these fields and my preference was less important.

When I was three years old, in 1938, I used to walk a lane like these lanes to Liosicarn School with my mother who taught there. We lived with her and our grandmother, our father's mother, in a small bungalow a mile outside the town of Ballinamore. Our father lived separately in the police barracks twenty miles away in Cootehall, where he was Sergeant. We spent the long school holidays with him in the barracks, and he came and went to the bungalow in his blue, baby Ford on annual holidays and the two days he had off in every month. Behind the bungalow was a steep rushy hill, and beside it a blacksmith's forge. The bungalow which we rented must have been built for the blacksmith and was a little way up from the main road that ran to Swanlinbar and Enniskillen and the North. The short pass from the road was covered with clinkers from the forge. They crunched like grated teeth beneath the traffic of hooves and wheels that came and went throughout the day. Hidden in trees and bushes on the other side of the main road was the lane that led to Liosicarn where my mother taught with Master Foran. Liosicarn had only a single room and the teachers faced one another when they taught their classes, the long benches arranged so that their pupils sat back to back, a clear space between the two sets of benches on the boarded floor. On the window sill glowed the blue Mercator globe, and wild flowers were scattered in jam jars on the sills and all about the room.

Master Foran, whose wife was also a teacher, owned a car, a big Model T Ford, and in wet weather my mother and I waited under trees on the corner of the lane to be carried to the school. In good weather we always walked. There was a drinking pool for horses along the way, gates to houses, and the banks were covered with all kinds of wild flowers and vetches and wild strawberries. My mother named these flowers for me as we walked, and sometimes we stopped and picked them for the jam jars. I must have been extraordinarily happy walking that lane to school. There are many such lanes all around where I live, and in certain rare moments over the years, while walking in these lanes, I have come into an extraordinary sense of security, a deep peace, in which I feel that I can live forever. I suspect it is no more than the actual lane and the lost lane becoming one for a moment in an intensity of feeling, but without the usual attendants of pain and loss. These moments disappear as suddenly and as inexplicably as they come, and long before they can be recognized and placed.

I don't think I learned anything at school in Liosicarn, though I had a copybook I was proud of. I was too young and spoiled, and spoiled further by the older girls in Liosicarn who competed in mothering me during the school breaks. I remember the shame and rage when they carried me, kicking and crying, into the empty schoolroom to my mother. Everybody was laughing: I had sat on a nest of pismires on the bank until most of the nest was crawling inside my short trousers.

Our grandmother had been a dressmaker and stood arrow-straight in her black dresses. My handsome father, who stood arrow-straight as well until he was old, was her only child. She had been a local beauty and was vain and boastful. She was forever running down the poor land of Leitrim and its poor-looking inhabitants, which must have done nothing for her popularity. It was true that my father's relatives were tall and many were handsome: 'When we went to your mother's wedding and saw all those *whoosins* from Cavan—Smiths and Leddys and Bradys and McGaherns—we felt like scrunties off the mountain,' my Aunt Maggie told me once laughingly.

The McGaherns set great store on looks and maleness and position. There was a threat of violence in them all, and some were not a little mad and none had tact.

There was a wonderful-looking first cousin of my father's, Tom Leddy, a guard like my father, who had also married a teacher. He was stationed at Glenfarne on the shores of Lough Melvin. Years later, out of the blue, he called soon after my father had remarried to find my stepmother alone in the house—a clever, plain-looking woman who adored my father and was both his slave and master. Having introduced himself forthrightly, he demanded, 'Who are you? Are you the new housekeeper?' 'I'm Frank's wife,' she responded. 'Frank's wife,' he looked at her in amazement, and broke into such uncontrollable laughter that he had to sit down. 'Frank's wife. That's the best one I've heard in years. The whole country must be going bananas.' When he rose, he repeated, 'Frank's wife. You have made my day. Well, whoever you are, tell Frank that his cousin Tom Leddy called and that I'll call soon again one of these years,' and left as abruptly as he came.

Whether my grandmother was a little mad as well, I was too young to know. She either had a great influence on my father or their temperaments were similar. They were both violent and wilful. Once, when she caught me burning bits of paper in the open grate of the small range to watch them blaze in the fascination children have with flame, she caught and thrust my finger between the glowing bars. She disregarded both my cries and my mother's horrified protestations. 'You have the child half ruined already. There's only one way he'll learn.' Neither she nor my father had any sense of humour, and they hardly ever smiled or laughed, and they looked on any manifestation of enjoyment in others as a symptom of irresponsibility. They also saw it as diverting attention from themselves. The difference between them was great as well. My father was intelligent and could be charming, even gallant, when he wanted. Though he was as vain and proud as she, he was never boastful: 'Nobody blows themselves up other than fools. If you need praise, get others to do it for you.'

I am sure my mother took me with her because she loved me and because I had become a nuisance in the house. I had three sisters already, the twins Breedge and Rosaleen and the infant Margaret, not much more than three years spanning all four of us. I was a single star until the twins arrived, and I became insanely jealous of the natural transfer of attention. On dry days, when my mother was at school, my grandmother often left the twins out in the sun between the house and the forge, high on the sloping pass of clinkers that ran to the open gate on the road. I was forever around the forge, and she would warn me to mind them before going back into the house, having locked the brake on their big pram. I must have been planning how to get them out of my life for some time. I learned to unlock the brake and one day, after careful checking that nobody was watching either from the forge or the house or the road, I pushed the pram down the slope. The pass wasn't steep and the wheels would have bumped and slowed on the clinkers, but before it came to a stop the pram wheeled off the pass and overturned. The twins weren't hurt, but all this time my grandmother had been observing me from behind a curtain, and made not the slightest attempt—she had only to tap the window—to protect the twins, though she was out of the house and able to seize me as I was watching the pram overturn in terrified dismay.

I saw this same calculating coldness in my father many times.

My mother was unusual in that she disliked using any form of physical punishment when it was routine and widespread and savage beatings were a commonplace in schools, but she had trouble with the inspectors over the lack of strict discipline in her classes. In those remote schools the teachers were expected to serve the inspector lunch, and I remember her anxiety as she prepared the lunch the night before, having bought rare delicacies such as ham and tomatoes. The demand that all the children of the State should be able to speak and write in Irish had been raised to a punitive level. If the classes were found to be less than proficient in Irish, the teacher could lose salary increments. This brought an added tension to the inspections and ensured that a great many school hours were wasted on the teaching of Irish, to the neglect of other subjects, at a time when most of the children would have to emigrate to Britain or America to find work. Such was her nature that she tried to put a good face on everything and to keep us from her own anxiety.

I haven't a single memory of my father staying in the bungalow, though he must have come many times in his blue, baby Ford. On the dashboard of the small car was a glass jar filled with long sugar sticks wrapped in cellophane. Most were yellow but some were green and red and black. I thought they were beautiful as well as desirable, but they were never unwrapped or given around and seemed to serve the same function as permanent flowers.

That I have not a single memory of my father in the house and that the lane to Liosicarn was walked alone with my mother would seem to conform to a certain primal pattern of the father and the son. The first memory I have of him in all that time would seem to reinforce this further. The memory is of a summer in the barracks in Cootehall. My grandmother, my mother, the twins and I must have gone there during the long school holidays.

I had a head of curls like a girl. My father decided to remove them in spite of my frightened protests, made worse by my mother and grandmother's obvious distress, which only served to strengthen his resolve. In his uniform with the three silver stripes of his rank on the blue sleeve, he took me out into the long hallway that ran along the stairs to the door of the dayroom. He took a chair and newspaper and the small silver shears from the green box and locked the two women into the living room.

This hallway was always dark, but there must have been light enough from the small window beneath the stairs. The chair was set down on the newspapers and it did not take long to remove the curls. Exultant, he brought me back into the living room, where my outraged cries must have added to the distress of the two women. He carried the curls in the folds of the newspaper. 'Weep not for me, O women of Jerusalem, but for yourselves and for your children,' he quoted triumphantly.

In trying to explain or excuse or ameliorate that open or latent sense of conflict that always lay between us at even the best of times, my sisters, who remained close to my father, used to say that after my birth he felt displaced in my mother's affections and was never able to forgive or come to terms with that hurt; but I am certain if that hadn't been there, something else would have been found. In turn, those brown curls in the folds of the newspaper came to resemble for me John the Baptist's severed head borne into the room on a silver plate. Religion and religious imagery were part of the air we breathed.

Prayers were said each morning. Work and talk stopped in fields and houses and school and shop and the busy street at the first sound of the angelus bell each day at noon. Every day was closed with the rosary at night. The worlds to come, hell and heaven and purgatory and limbo, were closer and far more real than America or Australia and talked about almost daily as our future reality.

Heaven was in the sky. My mother spoke to me of heaven as concretely and with as much love as she named the wild flowers. Above us the sun of heaven shone. Beyond the sun was the gate of heaven. Within the gates were the thrones and mansions, the Three Persons in the One God, the Blessed Virgin, the angels and saints, and beyond those mansions were the gardens of Paradise where time ceased and everything entered an instant of joy that lasted for all eternity at one with the mind of God. It was her prayer and fervent

MILES

0   10   20

DONEGAL·BAY

NORTHERN

IRELAND

SLIGO

ENNISKILLEN

SLIGO

LEITRIM

COOTEHALL

LEITRIM

BALLINAMORE

CARRICK-ON-SHANNON

DROMOD

BEAGHMORE

LOUGH·GOWNA

IRELAND

TO DUBLIN

RIVER

SHANNON

BELFAST

DUBLIN

hope that we would all live there together in happiness with God for all eternity. Heaven was in the sky. Hell was in the bowels of the earth. There, eternal fire raged. The souls of the damned had to dwell in hell through all eternity, deprived forever of the sight of the face of God. At its entrance was a great river. Across a wide plain, naked and weeping, came the souls of the damned from the Judgement Seat, bearing only a single coin to give to the boatman to take them across the river into eternal fire.

Between this hell and heaven, purgatory was placed. Descriptions of it were vague, probably because all of us expected to spend time there. The saints alone went straight to heaven. In purgatory, we would have to be purified in flame to a whiteness like that of snow before we could join the saints in the blessedness of heaven.

Away in a silent corner was limbo, where grave-faced children who hadn't received baptism slept, without consciousness or pain, throughout all eternity. Limbo was closed to us because of our baptism. In those young years, contemplating a future hell, or at best the long purifications of purgatory, it did not seem a bad place at all, and there were times when I hoped that some essential rite had been overlooked during my baptism; but I could not communicate this to my mother.

At Easter my mother always showed us the sun. 'Look how the molten globe and all the glittering rays are dancing! The whole of heaven is dancing in its joy that Christ has risen.' When Easter arrived with overcast skies and we asked for the sun, she assured us it was dancing behind the clouds. Blessed are those who have not seen but have believed.

At times in the evening the sun appeared within reach, when it stood in the whitethorns high on the hill behind the house before disappearing. I began to watch it as I had earlier eyed the bright battering at the forge. If I could climb the hill while it rested in the whitethorns, I could walk through the sun to the gate of heaven. Once I started to climb, it was like climbing a terrible stairs, having to claw and drag my way up through the rushes; but with every step the sun grew closer, and it was still there when I got to the whitethorns. I pushed through a hole in the hedge and rolled down into a dry drain. I intended to walk into the sun when I rose from the drain, but what confronted me was a mocking mirage: the sun was miles away, on the top of another hill. A long, flat plain of wheaten sedge lay between the two hills that would take days and hours to cross. I must have crawled or fallen back into the drain in a sleep of pure exhaustion.

It was dark when I woke to hear voices calling my name and saw stars bright in the sky. I was scolded and carried down to the house. Their anxiety changed to amusement and laughter and some wonder when they learned my story. I had tried to climb to the sun to get to the gate of heaven. I had not understood that you have to pass through death to reach that gate.

My grandmother had grown very possessive, and this must have been one of the reasons my mother took me with her on that lane to Liosicarn before I was of school-going age. When I went down with whooping cough my grandmother had her revenge. She shut me up in her own room and locked the door when she left the room. My mother did not see me for weeks. She had to go to school, my grandmother argued, and she and the twins and the infant Margaret couldn't be let run the risk of infection. As soon as the first wave of the illness passed, I became very distressed that I couldn't get to my mother nor she to me. I shouted and called out to her through the locked door. Even the rosary was said with the door locked. My mother counselled me to be patient and to pray that soon I'd be better and able to walk the lane to school again. In those weeks only once was I taken from the room.

There was a cure for the whooping cough that involved a mule or a jennet or a donkey. A neighbour of ours, Tommy Quinn, who spent any money he got on drink and was thought to be a little simple, lived with his brother Jim in a black house across the road in a rookery of trees. He came with the animal very late one night to the back door. I am sure the idea of the cure came from my grandmother and that Tommy came late at night so that the ritual could not be observed. The night was very cold. In a bundle of blankets I was taken out and passed beneath the jennet or mule or donkey three times in the name of the Father and the Son and the Holy Ghost. I remember the frost glistening on the hard ground and the sky was full of stars as I was handed back and forth. My happiness was intense when I was restored to my mother and we were walking the lane to Liosicarn together again.

John McGahern

Troubles with my grandmother did not cease; I was now her undisputed favourite, albeit a wary and unwilling one. She took to boasting about me in the same way she did about Cavan and the *whoosins* from there who were her relatives, the McGaherns and the Bradys and the Smiths and the Leddys. Though I was never to be handsome or tall, she would say of me, 'Sean has the brains of the world and can do anything.' My mother would have disliked this boasting and done everything she could to temper it.

One Saturday my grandmother decided to send me all the way into town to Aunt Maggie's shop for a packet of cornflakes. My mother protested that I was too young for such a long journey and offered to accompany me. My grandmother would have none of it: 'He's well able. He's far too mollycoddled. It's time he learned to strike out on his own.'

The town was a little less than a mile from the bungalow, and my aunt's shop was beside the railway station. Her brother, my Uncle Pat, who owned a hackney car, lived with her and met the trains with his car. She also kept lodgers, men who worked on the railway, firemen, drivers, repair linesmen, nearly all of them from Dublin. The shop sold sweets, chocolate, fruit, cigarettes, toys, groceries, schoolbooks and stationery. I was delighted at the prospect of getting away into the town on my own. I felt well able to make the journey and supported my grandmother.

There was no rain, and I arrived at the shop with the coins and a note from my mother. The errand was probably greeted with derision as soon as its source was discovered. I was fussed over, given biscuits or plum cake and tea in the delicious heat and comfort of the kitchen, before being sent on my way home with the packet of cornflakes. At Liosicarn I had watched enviously from the bank as the older boys played football, and my dream was to learn to play. Once I was clear of the town, I had a free road. There was no traffic, no carts, no bicycles, only a few people walking. As soon as they passed, I put the packet down and kicked it the whole way home— free kicks, kicks from the hand, kicks at goal. By the time I reached the bungalow, the packet wasn't recognizable. As soon as my grandmother saw it, she was beside herself. The beating would have been much worse but for my mother's intervention.

Soon after, and suddenly, my grandmother disappeared. She was there one day and gone the next. I must have accepted whatever explanation was given. She was there and then she was gone, and the days continued without her disappearance making any difference to our lives.

I was to see her one last time. One Sunday my father came for us in the Ford, the jar of wrapped sugar sticks on the dashboard like flowers. He was in the brown suit that had been tailored for his wedding day, which he wore for years afterwards. My mother was dressed in a long pleated woollen dress. Not only was this Sunday outing unusual but even more so was the shining care with which they were both dressed. We were told that the twins and I were going to Carrick-on-Shannon to visit our grandmother. Rosaleen and Breedge were dressed identically in cotton dresses of the same flowery material; even their hair was parted and combed in the same fashion and tied with the same colour of ribbon. Dressed like this, hardly anybody outside the family was able to tell them apart. I was in my summer Mass clothes—white shirt, short blue trousers, white ankle socks, polished black shoes. The car stopped at Aunt Maggie's shop, and mother got out to buy grapes and sweets. My father must have felt she was spending too much time with her sister in the shop because soon he was muttering and complaining aloud to us, and then he blew the horn. She was full of apologies when she came out, but he continued muttering to himself, driving away in an angry silence. There were many times, then and later, when Aunt Maggie and my father weren't speaking, and this must have been one of those times, for otherwise she would have come out to the car to greet us.

We drove through the town in silence, passing the big stone barracks by the bridge to which our father had come as a young sergeant when the Civil War was ending. By the canal on the outskirts of the town was the convent with the blue-and-white grotto of the Blessed Virgin that had been our mother's first school. The punishing silence was broken only when the spires of the churches came into view above the low roofs of Carrick. On a higher isolated hill stood a water tower, like a huge concrete mushroom, beside a grey stone building that was once the poorhouse and was now the hospital we were going to visit.

We walked down a long corridor before pausing outside a numbered door. My mother and father whispered together. They must have been afraid to face my grandmother. My father put the grapes into my hands. 'Sean, you go and see Granny first.'

The door opened. I saw her head on pillows and went toward her with the black grapes. She was glad to see me, and we kissed. The twins came next with the chocolates, and, a long time afterwards, my father and mother. All I remember of the rest of the visit was my grandmother's bitter complaints that they had put her in the poorhouse and left her to die. She wouldn't concede that it was a hospital or that she needed care. As we were leaving, she wanted to give back the grapes and chocolates, but my father insisted that they had been bought specially for her. He scolded her that she should make more of an effort to like the place, as she was being given great care. This was the only time I ever saw her cry. My mother took us out into the corridor and my father remained behind with her a long time.

Sometime afterwards, a Hail Mary for the repose of her soul was added to the prayers we said each night at the end of the Rosary. We said the prayer mechanically, as we said all prayers, without the words having any import or meaning.

A greater change now happened. The number of pupils fell in Liosicarn. At a time of harsh government cutbacks no new teachers were being employed. My mother was placed on the 'Panel'. All vacancies had to be filled from these panels, and the teachers had no choice but to move. The school was Beaghmore, close to Carrigallen, ten or eleven miles away. Unusually for the time, it had a woman principal, a large, pleasant woman who had married into a prosperous farm beside the school. We left the bungalow and moved into a stark two-storeyed house overlooking a bog near Cloone.

There was no running water then, other than in streams or rivers, no electricity, no TV, very few radios, and when newspapers were bought they were shared between houses. Each locality lived within its own small world, and moving to the house overlooking the bog was like moving to a different country. The war that had broken out all over Europe was a distant rumour. I remember vividly an excited man coming into the house and waving his arms around as he declared, 'German planes are manuring bombs all over England!'

My mother walked the two miles from the house to Beaghmore

in all weathers with the twins. By then I had a new baby sister, Monica, and she and Margaret were minded by the new maid. I walked in the opposite direction to Augharan School, no more than a half mile away on the road to Newtowngore. There were mornings I wished it was a hundred miles away.

For a long time, my father had been complaining that my mother spoiled me—that she spoiled us all—and he saw the closeness of Augharan as an opportunity for correction: I would be torn from my mother's petticoats and be made into a man in the natural harshness of the world. At Augharan he got his wish.

Mrs McCann was the junior teacher in Augharan. She was married to a tailor in Carrigallen and cycled to and from the town each day. She kept a supply of bright yellow canes in the press, and when they splintered she used ash and sally and hazel from the hedges and plied them with zeal all through the day, for errors and mistakes, oral or written, for any straying of attention or the slightest indiscipline. The worst punishments were administered out in the corridor, away from the classroom.

I probably wasn't beaten any more than the other children, but I wasn't used to being beaten, and after my mother's gentleness it was a descent into hell. I tried fiercely to leave Augharan and go with her and the twins to Beaghmore, but to no avail.

My father stood behind the decision. Whether it was because we were older and more aware, he seemed to be coming more often to the house. Talk of the war in Britain and Europe was now constant, and I made a silent, fervent prayer of my own each night after the Rosary that God in His mercy would send one of the German planes over England astray in the night to manure a bomb on Augharan School while we slept.

I doubt if Mrs McCann was unusually violent for that time. I have seen men my own age grow strange with anger when recalling their schooling: 'Often we wouldn't be able to hold tools in the evenings, our hands would be that black and swollen. They'd often pull across the legs or the arms and shoulders. How we learned anything was a mystery. Heading out to school each day was pure misery.'

I am sure there were exceptions, but once anything is licensed it can grow monstrous and be scarcely noticed. The only recourse for parents then was to come to the school to complain or go to the priest, or threaten law, but that was rare. Authority's writ ran from God the Father down and could not be questioned. Violence reigned as often as not in the homes as well. One of the compounds at its base was sexual sickness and frustration, as sex was seen, officially, as unclean and sinful, allowable only when it too was licensed. Doctrine separated body and soul. The soul was eternal and belonged to God. The body that carried it was unclean and prone to sin and would die, though I doubt if Mrs McCann was concerned with this division as she plied her canes and hazels.

Since all my attempts to get away had come to nothing, I turned now to see if I could chance on anything that might woo her to my side. On the way to school was a little garden by an abandoned cottage. Someone had enriched and cultivated it once, but it was neglected now and wild, rank with thistle and nettle and briar and dock. I developed the habit of looking at the wild flowers along the way on my own, just as my mother and I had paused and named them together on the lane to Liosicarn. It might also have been a way of delaying my arrival at Augharan, but I thought the purple of the thistle blossoms were especially beautiful, lovely as roses. A small wooden gate opened into the garden, and I thought that if I could beat my way into the tall growth I would be able to gather a big bunch of the purple blossoms to take to Mrs McCann. By the time I had a small bunch picked, I was stung with nettles and my hands and legs were bloodied from the crawling briars. Perhaps not recognizing the thistles immediately, Mrs McCann took the bunch of purple blossoms in amazement, but as soon as she felt the thorns and recognized the despised weed, she grew enraged. What did I think I was doing bringing thistles to the school? Who did I think she was? Was I making fun of her and the school? She had never seen the like. She ordered me to throw the thistles out before she lost control of herself. I returned to the classroom humiliated, knowing that my attempt at ingratiation had only worsened my position. If I wasn't able to find knowledge of this shameful abasement within myself, I had only to look around at the sly, knowing smiles of my classmates.

My humiliation was further deepened when I told my mother what had happened. I showed her my torn legs and wrists, the nettle stings, but when I finished she was unable to stop laughing and was joined by my sisters. I was about to run from the house when she drew me to her. I had only another month to go till my first communion, she told me. If I learned my catechism well and received my first confession and communion, I could then leave Augharan and go with her and the twins to Beaghmore. I was barely able to believe my good fortune.

Mrs McCann's husband made the blue suit for my first communion. The evening before, my mother had taken me to the dark church of Aughavas where my first confession was heard. That night Mr McCann came on a motorbike to our house above the bog with the tailored blue suit. I wore it the next morning with a white shirt and white ankle socks in new shoes. The farm next to the house where we bought milk had a big sidecar. There wasn't a place for my mother, but I was given a seat in front with the driver. My mother cycled to the church. I had never felt so high up before and was too terrified to look down at the road or the horses' hooves as the hedges flew past. Mrs McCann was in the church, and she shepherded the class to our seats and then to the altar rail, where, with closed eyes, we received from the priest the white wafer that was the Body and Blood of Christ. I was made much of afterwards. People gave me coins that were heavy and jingled when I shook the pockets of my new blue suit. As we came home on the sidecar, I was less afraid and began to enjoy the height and wide view in my newfound grace. If I fell now and died, I would go straight to heaven. I had been fasting from the night before and was starving. A royal feast waited in the house: a mug of steaming tea, a plate of buttered toast, a fried egg, pork sausage, two slices of grilled bacon and a piece of black pudding. 'Daddy wrote that he'd love to be here but wasn't able to get off,' our mother said.

The next morning I did not have to turn away and face for Augharan when we got to the road. In pure relief and happiness, I reached out and took my mother's hand as she and I and the twins set out for Beaghmore.

All these roads were dirt roads that ran between wild hedges studded with mature trees—ash or oak or sycamore—and high grass margins. The road from the house reached the wider road to Carrigallen. We crossed a stone bridge and then turned up the short lane to the school.

John McGahern

Beaghmore had two classrooms but no porch and was on the lane; it had no playground, just space for the two dry lavatories beneath the tall boundary hedge at the back. The playground was a field on the other side of the lane where we played ball and ran and jumped amid the grazing, incurious cattle.

The woman principal became very friendly with my mother. I remember her comfortable pleasantness but not her name, while I can never forget Mrs McCann. Her house was close to the school and we were often invited there, and on many Friday evenings we stayed for tea. When we left, we were often given pots of jam or preserves or eggs and fresh vegetables or material that could be made into children's clothes. The two women would sit and chat while we listened without understanding or wandered out into the farmyard. There was a big concreted yard with walls and gates, sheds full of pigs and cattle, a house for fowl, a stable with three horses, ploughs and harrows, mowing machines, mangles, tedders, rakers. What I came away with was a sense of plenty, warmth and ease and comfort, even luxury set against the bareness of our rented rooms. I took this same sense away from most of the houses we visited, together with a vague troubled feeling of shame and diminishment.

'Why can't we have a house like those houses, Mammy?'

'Maybe one day we will—but money and comfort isn't everything. When people are rich it is often harder for them to leave the world.'

'Does it mean it is harder for them to get to heaven?'

'If they come to love the world too much it is harder. God is more important than the world and He sees all.'

Our close neighbours were our most constant visitors, dropping in at all sorts of times throughout the day, as was usual then—to be passing the house was reason enough—and they sometimes came at night to sit around the fire. The other visitors we had were all relatives of my father's. His home place near Gowna was not far from Carrigallen, and he encouraged them to visit us, though he'd be far from happy if they took to visiting him. I suspect that he viewed them as a counterweight to my mother's relatives, whom he resented. They were, for the most part, young women who would cycle over to us from Gowna in the evening, stay the night and leave with us when we set out for school in the morning. Secretly, my mother did not welcome these visits, but neither did she stand in their way, and when

John McGahern's mother (right) with friends

John McGahern

they came she put them at their ease and made them welcome.

Of the young girls and women who cycled over to us from Gowna, I remember a close cousin of my father's, perhaps because of her beauty—she had very pale skin and black hair—but it is more likely that the memory is fixed by an incident on the way to school. As we walked to school in the morning, the girl wheeling her bicycle on her way home after staying the night, my mother quietly excused herself and turned aside. A grey stream poured from her mouth into the long grass and nettles growing on the margins of the road.

'It's only early morning sickness,' she explained to the girl when she had composed herself and resumed the walk. The girl nodded and asked some further question, and the walk and conversation continued normally as if nothing had happened. In spite of this, I was touched by a strange foreboding, but was too fearful to ask anything.

I felt the same fear when my father was in the house. I knew he resented that I had been given my way over Augharan and Mrs McCann. There was always tension when he was in the house, scolding about how money was being wasted, or the poor way the house was being run, or my mother's relatives. In certain moods he did not need a reason to fall into a passion of complaint, which then fed off its own anger. A child can pick up unhappiness like a virus. This was further worsened by a scene that reached back to the shearing of my head of curls beneath the stairs in the barrack hallway. Late at night the small blue car arrived with my father in one of his black moods. This focused instantly on my face, which was covered with scabs from a childhood disease, probably impetigo. In the morning he kept me from school and drove me to the doctor in Carrigallen. He had a love/hate relationship with doctors, and though we spent a long time in the surgery and there was much argument, I was too afraid and confused to know what was happening. From the surgery we went straight to the chemist's, probably for an antiseptic lotion or ointment. When he got home he ordered Bridgie McGovern to boil water, got a basin and mirror and towel and sharp knife, disinfected the water and knife. Then he proceeded to remove all the scabs with the knife. I was terrified of him—the knife, the ceremony that was as fixed as an execution.

The treatment worked, the sores healed, and the knife left no scars, but the next time I saw the blue, baby Ford arrive I ran to a big chestnut tree we were used to climbing near the house, and I hid there. I was able to observe the house and the car, and though I heard my name called out, I remained in the tree. Towards evening the car left, the calling became more anxious and constant, and I went into the house.

The next time he came to the house he was at his most charming. He had a physical attractiveness that practically glowed when he was in this humour, but seldom was he able to sustain it: he demanded that the whole outside world should reflect it perfectly back. Once this mirror dimmed or failed, his mood would turn. On this day in the stark house above the bog, we must have responded perfectly because the house was filled with contentment and peace all through the day and into the night and morning, until we gathered outside the house to wave to the car as he drove away.

A few weeks later the world of Beaghmore was ended. Mother suddenly had to go away. For what or why we were not told. 'You all have to be good now and cause no trouble and pray for Mammy.' Faces were grave and anxious and closed against questioning. The house above the bog was closed. All five of us and Bridgie McGovern were moved to the barracks in Cootehall. The rooms in the living quarters had been uninhabited for so long, other than by my single father and a maid, that they gave back our voices when we shouted out. This shouting soon got on his nerves down in the dayroom: he opened the dayroom door and roared up at us to have manners, to be quiet and remember that we were no longer living in a field.

The village of Cootehall was scattered randomly about a big triangular field, Henry's field. No two shops or houses adjoined one another, and they were set down as haphazardly as if they had been carried there on various breezes. There was a church, a post office, the barracks, a presbytery, two shops, three bars, a few houses. A row of buildings, all owned by Michael Henry—stables, cowhouses, a granary, a bar, a dwelling house, a grocery store—stood across a narrow lane from the church wall.

The school stood just outside the village and was relatively new, with concrete shelters in the playground. Mrs Finan and Mrs Mullaney shared the junior classroom. They were severe and of their time, but neither was as violent as Mrs McCann. We learned to dread

John McGahern

Mrs Finan's wedding and engagement rings when she used her fist.
They were handsome women, Mrs Finan some years the younger.
Mrs Mullaney was a junior assistant—she had never been formally
trained—and wasn't as assured professionally or socially as Mrs
Finan, who was married to a teacher and had two brothers who were
priests. Mrs Mullaney had a will of iron. She had a boy and a girl
by her first husband. Under her fierce tutelage, they had both won
scholarships and were now in college. Her second husband, Mr
Mullaney, was old, but fame of sorts clung to him as a horseman—
he was said to have cleared dangerous and almost impossible gates
and ditches when young. Once they married, he sold his farm and
built her a bungalow beside the church. Each day he brought her a
hot lunch to the school, traces of his early horsemanship showing in
his walk as he made his slow way with the dishes between the
bungalow and the school. Mrs Mullaney was prominent in all things
connected with the church, and it was assumed that both her son and
daughter were being driven towards the priesthood and the convent.

   The Principal was Master Glynn, a gentle, easy-going alcoholic.
The two women teachers both protected and managed him. He had
entered teaching as a monitor in the British system, but had never
managed to learn any Irish after Independence, when even the letter
boxes acquired a coat of green paint. When Irish had to be taught
to his classes, he and Mrs Finan swapped rooms. Those were very
pleasant times when he came to our room, as he generally gave Mrs
Finan's classes copying work and passed the time chatting with Mrs
Mullaney. Most teachers used their foothold in education to better
their children in the world, getting them into the church or the
professions or the civil service through their knowledge of the
examination system, but Master Glynn's large family had all returned
to the land in much the same way as uncultivated fields return to
the wilderness. Now they were no different in ambition or interests
or social standing than most of the parents of the children he taught.
His easy-going nature combined with heavy drinking had become a
disability. A gang of older boys, who were out of control and did
more or less whatever they wanted, locked him in one of the
cloakrooms. When released by the women teachers, who caned the
ringleaders within an inch of their lives, he foolishly sent to the
barracks for the Guards to come to the school and restore order. My

32

father had nothing but contempt for the weakness of such a man. He went down to the trees growing on the river bank, cut an ash plant and sent it back to the master with a note giving detailed, ironic instructions for its use.

Every night Master Glynn went to Henry's bar, where he was popular with his old pupils. If he had never taught them much, neither had he ever abused them, and many of them were still able to quote reams of Goldsmith from his tutelage. As the drinks flew round, he assured them of the great intelligences they all possessed, and they in their turn told him that he was the best teacher any class of scholars ever had and how they remembered as if it was yesterday everything he had ever taught them. Their voices brimming with emotion, another round of drinks was called and, 'A large brandy for the Master!'

Cootehall was my fourth school in as many years. We were new and stood out, but we were also from the barracks. In the Ireland of that time the law was still looked upon as alien, to be feared and avoided, and kept as far away from as possible. This conferred on us an ambiguous protection that was paper thin.

Up to now our mother had always been with us. Now that she was gone we were at the mercy of our father's scoldings, and sudden rages, and beatings. In their surviving letters my father often complains to my mother that she is turning us against him, when it was he himself who was turning us away from him. While, in fits, he could charm and seduce us, when we did go towards him he found us tiresome and could not sustain what he had brought about. The protection our mother gave had not always been without danger to herself.

There were two entrances to the living quarters: through the long hallway from the stairs and dayroom or by the back door through the scullery. The back door opened on a small concrete yard. Across the yard was the slated house my father used as a workshop. There was a water barrel under the eve pipe and a turf shed beyond and across from the open turf shed, towards the river was a slated lavatory. It was dark within, and instinctively we ran to its darkness after beatings. Between the shed and the lavatory was a rough lawn with a rhubarb bed in its centre. In the summer, butterflies, especially white butterflies, seemed to endlessly flicker and flit and toss in the light above this bed, sometimes alighting and taking off from the great rhubarb leaves. Often we tried to close our hands on these flickering lights.

Margaret was the most wilful of the girls, with a stubborn energy, and was then, and later, always the one most likely to cross my father. I remember a day when we were to see my father in Cootehall, before we moved there and our mother was still with us. Margaret ran from the house, pursued by my father in full uniform. The day was heavy and hot and still. Beyond the netting-wire, where the tarred boat was moored below the barracks, the river did not seem to move. All the doors were open. We were gathered at the back around our mother. Margaret could not have been much more than three at the time. My mother did not so much move as just stand in his way as the child went past. He was in such a passion that he didn't pause, but drew out to send her spinning into the rhubarb beds. She did not fall but reached down into the rhubarb stalks for support before getting to her feet. My father caught the child before she reached the lavatory and lifted and shook her violently. She was too paralysed to kick or cry out, and eventually he put her down without further chastisement.

'God. O God, O God,' he began. 'You'd think those children were brought up in a field!'

He seemed to have no sense of what he had done or that my mother might be hurt.

'They are very young,' she said.

'There's no peace since they came. You'd hear them in Boyle, never mind down in the barracks. No peace or work can get done with their constant racket.'

Now my mother was gone and there was only Bridgie McGovern. She cooked and washed and sewed for my father and us and minded Monica when the rest of us were at school. She was a young, attractive woman, flirtatious and egotistical. My sisters say she used to flirt with my father, and there is little doubt they got on well together.

The three men attached to the barracks were Guard Guider, Guard Murray and Guard Cannon. They were all married and lived in rented houses. The Guiders, who were from Tipperary, had the largest family, ten or twelve children, and they lived in a big slated house beside the quay that belonged to the Water Authority. One of the Guider children, Tom, had a heart condition, and rode to school on a donkey. His father was fond of saying that if Christ could ride in to Jerusalem on an ass, it was no disgrace for a Guider to ride to school on the same animal. Later the Guiders were transferred and replaced by a newly married couple, the Walshes, who in turn were to have many children. The Murrays lived in a huge stone house that had once been a British military barracks and was later torn down for its stone and slates and lead. Guard Murray was from Virginia in Cavan. He was gentle and humorous, anxious to please. His sharp, ambitious wife from Mayo ran him and their five children. The Cannons, recently married, were both from Donegal, he from the Gaeltacht. Teresa Cannon was often in the barracks. She was tall and handsome and sweet on my father. The Cannons had rooms in Lenihan's Bawn, their living room the surviving corner tower of Coote's Castle, which was supposed to be haunted by, among other things, a turkey cock with spurs. Mrs Cannon was afraid to sleep there alone when her husband was barrack orderly, and for years my sisters had to go to sleep with her on those nights in the Bawn. She was hypocritical and disliked, especially by women. 'I am fluent in two languages and haven't a word to say in either,' her husband was fond of boasting; 'while my wife doesn't even know her own language and has enough to say for six people.' He had worked as a shoemaker and then as a bus conductor in Glasgow before joining the guards. He was older than his wife, bald and very gentle when he wasn't on the tear. When he was barrack orderly and my father wasn't in the house, he would often leave the dayroom door open and sit with us in the big living room, chatting away as if his world and ours were the very same. Whenever there was a football match on the BBC, he stood for hours with his ear glued to the Cossor, trying to pick up the faint, crackling sounds as they came over the air from Scotland or England.

The barracks itself was a strange place, like most of the country at the time. Though the Free State had been wrested in armed conflict from Britain, it was like an inheritance that nobody quite understood or knew how to manage. The Catholic Church was dominant and in control of almost everything, directly or indirectly. In a climate of suppression and poverty and fear, there was hardly any crime and little need of a barracks in a place like Cootehall, other than as a symbol.

The place was run on lines that were no longer connected to any reality, if indeed they ever were. Though my father slept every night in the barracks, the guards in their turn had to leave their own family and sleep the night beside the telephone that hardly ever rang, even in the daytime. I cannot remember anybody coming to the barracks at night. If there was a sudden death or illness, people went to the priest, or to the doctor if they weren't poor.

The familiar sounds each night were the heavy boots of the barrack orderly taking down the bedclothes from the upstairs room to make up his bed for the night beside the phone. We'd hear the sounds of raking and blowing as he started the fire in the morning and then the unlocking of the back door when he went down to empty his pot and bucket of ashes into the ash pit over the river. We were able to tell the different guards by their sounds and footsteps. Sometimes in the mornings they hummed or whistled, which always set my father muttering.

My father would come down the stairs in his shirt and trousers and unlaced boots. The fire had to be going by then, the kettle boiling. We went through these mornings on tiptoe. While he sharpened his open razor on a leather strap that hung from the wall, we'd pour the shaving water into a basin that stood in a tall, rusted, iron stand in front of the scullery window. Then he would lather his face with a small brush and shave in the mirror that stood in a brown wooden stand in the window. Outside were the beds of rhubarb and beyond the low wall the shapes of Lenihan's fields.

The house went completely still while he shaved. Sometimes he would nick himself with the razor and we'd bring him bits of newspaper to staunch the bleeding. A clean, dry towel had to be placed in his hands as soon as he washed. In the living room he would polish and lace up his boots, draw the silver buttons of his tunic together on a flat, brass comb while he wetted them with a white substance, and brushed them till they shone. As soon as he buttoned his tunic, he would comb his hair in the big sideboard mirror. The signal that he was completely dressed was when he picked up his new handkerchief from the table and placed it inside the cuff that wore the three silver stripes of his rank. Then he would sit down to breakfast, facing the sideboard mirror. At this time Bridgie McGovern would have served him, later my sisters. He never acknowledged the server or any of the small acts of service, but would erupt into complaint if there was a fault—a knife or dish or fork or spoon missing, or something accidentally spilled or dropped.

When he wasn't eating from his plate, he stared straight ahead into the big mirror, chewing very slowly. At exactly nine he would go down to the dayroom, and the whole of the living room relaxed as soon as the dayroom door slammed shut.

The morning inspection took place in the dayroom, the three policemen lined up in front of my father on the far side of the long wooden table. Occasionally voices were raised and we would go silent to try to listen. The patrols for the day were assigned and written into one of the big ledgers on the table. The new orderly took over from the old, who was then free to go home to his own house and breakfast.

The new orderly's first task was to take the bottle from the copper rain-gauge in the garden, measure the rainfall in a long glass vial, and write the measurement on a chart that was sent at the end of each month to the meteorological office in Dublin. As soon as the green mail van crossed the bridge, a guard went to collect the mail, if there was any, and the *Irish Independent* from Charlie Reagan's. At that time the *Independent* printed the death notices on the front page. They were read out aloud. In a small country, with all the guards coming from different parts, on most mornings they would have some connection with one or more of the deceased, and the person or persons and their localities would be discussed. Then the headlines and any interesting news would be gone over while the newspaper was passed around. When all that was achieved, they scattered out on their different patrols, leaving the barrack orderly in charge in the dayroom. If there was wind and rain or heavy rain, they would hang about the dayroom looking out at the rain, and after a few hours they'd sign themselves back in and write up a fictitious account of the patrol without having left the dayroom.

Most of the accounts that were written into the big ledgers, in good weather and in bad, were fictitious, and were referred to laughingly as Patrols of the Imagination, but never by my father. Many of the patrols they cycled out on were spent working in their gardens or conacre or on their plots of turf on Gloria Bog. Only when the monthly inspection from the superintendent was due or a surprise inspection feared were the patrols observed and reported properly. Even then some invention was probably needed, as hardly anything ever happened other than tyre punctures on the potholed roads.

As I grew older I sometimes helped with the writing of the reports while hanging about the dayroom when my father was away.

'Would you ever put your head out the door, Sean, and see what way the wind is blowing?'

'It is from the priest's boathouse, Guard Cannon, with bits of rain.'

'Wind from the southwest, and beginning to rain. Everything quiet,' Guard Cannon would call out as he wrote in the big ledger. 'Everything still quiet until I reached Knockvicar,' he continued. 'Then I found a cow grazing along the road as soon as I turned for Cootehall. I made enquiries and discovered that the said animal belonged to Patrick McLoughlin. The owner denied any knowledge of the cow and said that if it was his it must have broken through a fence. I warned him as to the dangers of having an animal trespassing on the public highway and that I'd be forced to take further measures if the trespass was to occur again. Paper never refuses ink, Sean,' Guard Cannon would shout out as he concluded with a flourish: 'What is a masterpiece, Sean? A masterpiece is the correct distribution of ink on the correct number of white pages!'

What work did they do? Occasionally they summoned people for not having lights on their bicycles at night, for after-hours drinking, for assault, or trespass, owning unlicensed dogs, possessing fields of thistle, ragwort or dock. This came under the Noxious Weeds Act, which was printed on a framed poster that sometimes stood outside the porch on good days. There was a small bounty for dead foxes, and they cut the tongues out of the foxes brought to the barracks so that they couldn't be returned for further bounty. Occasionally, old and starving animals, mostly donkeys, were found abandoned on the roads, and they were brought in shivering to lie among the three circular flowerbeds on the barrack lawn until they were collected by the Burnhouse lorry. When the lorry arrived, they were pushed/carried on to the lorry, where they were shot by a humane killer. Once the shot rang out, the creatures crumpled to the floor of the lorry more silently than leaves.

I was seven years old during this first long stay in the barracks, and my whole childish world had been overturned. We didn't know where our mother was or what had happened to her and we were under our father's direct rule for the first time.

We come from darkness into light and grow in the light until at death we return to that original darkness. Those early years of the light are also a partial darkness because we have no power or understanding and are helpless in the face of the world. This is one of the great miseries of childhood. Mercifully, it is quickly absorbed by the boundless faith and energy and the length of the endlessly changing day of the child. Not even the greatest catastrophe can last the whole length of that long day.

We grow into an understanding of the world gradually. Much of what we come to know is far from comforting, that each day brings us closer to the inevitable hour when all will be darkness again, but even that knowledge is power and all understanding is joy, even in the face of dread, and cannot be taken from us until everything is. We grow into a love of the world, a love that is all the more precious and poignant because the great glory of which we are but a particle is lost almost as soon as it is gathered.

We were light years from that knowledge as we moved between Mrs Mullaney's classroom and the Church and the barracks. We had no power and no knowledge.

When I saw my mother again it was as if my lost world was restored and made whole and given back. Pat had come to the barracks for me in his car. We drove straight to Aughawillian and the poor-looking house that was to be our new home. I hardly saw anything when we got out of the car at the little iron gate on the road, so great was my longing. It was half day in the town, and Maggie had cycled out to be with my mother after school. They heard the car and came outside. I could hardly believe the joy that my eyes were seeing, and instinctively drew back and grew so self-conscious that I was barely able to walk beside my uncle down the new path of cinders. Not until I was nearer did I give way and run towards her until I was in her arms. Maggie teased me about my loss of words because of always talking too much and asking too many questions. I was ashamed that I was weeping.

Inside, a big fire of branches was blazing in the open hearth. Above it a kettle hung from a black iron rail that swung. Maggie brought a sweet cake from the town and tea was made.

'They are all the best in the barracks,' Pat said as we drank the tea and ate the sections of cake. 'They'll be down next week.'

John McGahern

I could taste nothing, neither tea nor cake, with the relief that she was back again and that I could touch her sleeve if I reached out. She was smiling and happy in her quiet way, while being attentive to everything, but there were times too when she looked close to tears.

'I heard you were a good boy and caught big fish with Daddy in the boat.'

'We caught severals.'

'And you had new teachers?'

'None of us liked the school. They were very hard. We did not know where you were. We were beginning to be afraid you might never come back.'

'I was in hospital,' she said quietly. 'I was sick and had to be there on my own for them to make me better. I hope you prayed for me.'

Maggie went outside and Pat climbed the short wooden stairs to look at the bedrooms.

'Every night we prayed for you at the Rosary, and I prayed for you on my own. For God to send you home to us again.'

'It's not a mansion, this house, but it's our own,' she said. 'The land is good. There are fine meadows.'

'We won't have to move and we'll be able to have animals?'

'Our moving is over. I'm permanent in Aughawillian.'

When Maggie returned, she was unusually quiet. The bedroom floors were so thin that we could hear every sound Pat made in the bedrooms.

'They're drying!' he said when he came down. 'The back room is good.'

'The gutters helped, and the windows—it's good we got them painted while the weather was dry.'

I wheeled Maggie's bicycle up the cinder footpath to the car on the road. Pat put the back wheel of the bicycle into the boot and secured it with rope. The two women embraced before Maggie got into the car.

'I'll be out tomorrow evening to see how the two of yous are getting on if I don't have too many runs to do off the train,' Pat said awkwardly before he got into the car.

'Don't worry,' my mother said. 'You have done far, far too much for us already,'

I was light-headed with happiness as I watched the car drive away.

My beloved was home and I was alone with her. The evening was clear and dry, the leaves yellow and fallen, and there was a burning red sun on the rim of the sky. We looked at the upstairs rooms, the two small bedrooms off the narrow landing, the larger bedroom where we'd sleep that night. The windowsills were low and deep enough to sit in. The ceiling boards were fixed to the rafters, only a few inches beneath the slates, and took on the shape of the roof. In wind and rain these frail rooms were thrilling at night because they brought us so close to the storm and yet kept us warm and sheltered and safe.

We walked the land together, going first through the meadows around the house. There was a spring well in the long meadow that ran to the woods. By a wooden plank we crossed into the small rough fields of the hill in front of the house.

She spoke of the hospital, of two trained singers who were patients in the ward and sang for them in the evenings, of how she made friends with Mrs Flanagan, whose son Paddy was a priest. Out of the close friendship my mother formed with Mrs Flanagan, her dream for me took shape, and I in turn took it up and gave it a further childish shape, until it was impossible to tell to whom the dream belonged.

One day, like Paddy Flanagan, I would become a priest. After the Ordination Mass I would place my freshly anointed hands in blessing on my mother's head. We'd live together in the priest's house and she'd attend each morning Mass and take communion from my hands. When she died, I'd include her in all the Masses that I'd say until we were united in the joy of heaven, when time would cease as we were gathered into the mind of God. There was no provision for my father or any of my sisters. Was the dream selfishly mine, or was it her dream, or was it a confusion of our different dreams? When she asked me, as she often did, 'Who do you love most of all?' I would answer readily and truthfully, 'You, Mother,' and despite her pleasure, she would correct me.

'You know that's not right, though it makes me glad.'

I love God most of all was the required response.

'And after God?'

'Mary, my mother in heaven.'

'And after Mary?'

'You, Mother.'

'You know that's not right either.'

'I love my earthly father and mother equally.'

The part of the dream that did not include my father must have been mine alone.

We walked to Ollarton's with a can for milk. We wore coats, as the night had turned cold under a clear, pale moon. We passed Brady's pond where the horses drank. Across from the pond was Brady's house and the smaller house where the old Mahon brothers lived. At the railway bridge we turned. An avenue of great trees lead up to Ollarton's, and in front of the house was a small lake ringed with reeds, still and clear as a mirror, reflecting the pale moon. When we entered the yard behind the house, we could hear them milking, which they interrupted when they saw us waiting with our can in the doorway. It was characteristic of my mother that she would have neither coughed nor spoken. By the light of a lantern milk was strained and measured into our can from a long-handled metal cup. The happiness of that walk and night under the pale moon was so intense that it brought on a light-headedness. It was as if the whole night, the dark trees, the moon in the small lake, moonlight making pale the gravel of the road we walked, my mother restored to me and giving me her free hand which I swung heedlessly were all filled with healing and the certainty that we'd never die. I was safe in her shadow. My chattering at times grew so wild that Mother let go of my hand and placed her fingers on my lips in reproof and amusement and love.

□

GRANTA

THE MERRY WIDOW
Edmund White

Lila Mae c. 1930

My mother was born Delilah Mae Teddlie in Texas at the beginning of the century. Her father, Jim Teddlie, was a railroad johnny, one of those men who repaired track or laid it. He died when my mother was seven or eight. She used to say he died of malaria while working in the swamps around Houston, but she had a postcard from him which he'd sent from a hospital in Colorado; perhaps he had tuberculosis. Was TB a more shameful disease than malaria? Was it the Aids of its day?

Mother always thought the loss of her father when she was still a child had instilled in her a floating, but permanent, dread of being abandoned by a man, a crucial man, or just by men, men in general. She had a very posed photo of her straight-nosed, square-jawed, wavy-haired father, looking no more than twenty-seven, in a rocking chair, while her full-faced ageless mother, Willie Lulu, hovered behind him in clean, copious laces, her glossy hair pulled back in a bun. She was standing and he sitting, the reverse of the usual positions for men and women in that day and age. My mother's brother, Jack, stood off to one side in short pants, with freckles and anger written all over his face. Beside him in a blur was my tiny mother as a five year old with a big, vague, white bow in her hair; the blur seemed to have been generated by the intensity of her feelings—or by a sudden movement. I'm sure that even then she never stood still.

She met my father in Texas and then they moved north, where I was born in Cincinnati. They were married twenty-two years— and then my father left my mother for his secretary. After the divorce, Mother moved my sister and me first to Evanston, Illinois, then to Dallas. She wanted to be near her folks in Texas and their town of Ranger was just a half day's drive away. I can still picture Lila Mae standing in front of her mother and stepfather in Ranger with a scarily bright smile on her face as she explained how wonderfully everything was going to turn out. She worked (in Evanston, then in Dallas, later in Rockford, Illinois) as a state psychologist. For a small salary she drove long distances from one primary school to another, testing all the children, on the lookout for those who were 'exceptional' (very bright or very slow) or handicapped in some way and in need of special training. She carried with her her testing materials in a brown leather attaché case. At night, she'd perch her reading glasses on the tip of her nose and grade dozens and dozens of IQ tests and personality tests.

Her mother had married again, to a Mr Snider, and the couple lived in a small, three-room house with a double bed in the living room. Mr Snider would sit in his big upholstered chair with the fan trained on his heavy body. Willie Lulu, constantly shaking almost as if sitting were a penance and she needed to stay in perpetual motion to remain in working order, would sit on the edge of their double bed. Every time she tried to get up to fetch more iced tea or bring out the peach ice cream she'd been churning all afternoon, Lila Mae would stop her. 'Mother,' she'd say, 'now you just sit still because I have something very, very important to tell you.'

Then Lila Mae would stand in her absurdly fashionable and expensive clothes she'd bought at Neiman-Marcus, stiff and brocaded and sweat-stained under the arms, her short, squat body bedecked one season in the New Look with its ballooning, crinolined skirts, the next season in the Trapeze Look, cut on the bias. These Paris couture styles looked as unlikely as kabuki costumes in the hot, humble Ranger house—beside Mr Snider with his collarless blue-and-white-striped shirt unbuttoned sufficiently to reveal his undershirt, his unbending wooden leg propped up on an ottoman and Willie in her loose housedress and carpet slippers, the baggy sleeves of her dress revealing her jiggly arms, fidgeting on the bed. Lila Mae would be wearing her high heels and nylons, attached under her skirt to the garters that dangled from her fat-crushing girdle. She owned no casual clothes—no shorts or halter tops, no trousers or T-shirts, no denim. Nothing except these costumes as costly and constricting as ceremonial kimonos. Though she was just five feet tall she weighed 160 or even 170 pounds, which her dramatic dresses emphasized. She'd been given a quick make-up course by a salesgirl at Neiman's and now she wore her eyebrows plucked and pencilled brown. Her cheeks were clown red, her eyelids smudged a faint blue. Above the right corner of her mouth was a large white mole that she thought of as a beauty mark. When Mother was in her twenties, a doctor had burned this mole but instead of dropping off it had just faded from its original black.

She'd say to Willie Lulu, 'Please, Mother, listen to my plan, because I'm going to go places in this world. I always try to present the best appearance possible, I never let myself just go, I've got my fine new Packard and brother!'—Here she shook her fists and let her face go radiant—'Just watch me go!'

'That's right, Sister, I always did say you're going to go places,' Willie said, smiling to herself, almost embarrassed that she'd taken the floor, though she meant to be nothing more than the Greek chorus to Lila Mae's protagonist. She called her own daughter 'Sister' and Jack 'Brother', just as our mother called my sister Margaret and me 'Sister' and 'Brother'. I guess it was a Southern custom but I imagined it derived from all those years Willie had lived alone with her children before her second marriage, just as my sister and I were our mother's only companions—siblings more than children.

People back then didn't have friends. They surrounded themselves with the families they'd been born into or had acquired through marriage. They knew many professional acquaintances, of course, and entertained them lavishly, but though they might become boozily chummy during an out-of-town convention, they never confided in one another and they did nothing to intensify these relationships. Mother would befriend people she met through her work but she always referred to them as 'the little people'. She'd say, 'I'm always very warm and open with the little people but I have to keep my distance or else they'd eat me alive.' She'd say with serene, unreflecting complacency, 'The little people just love me. No wonder. I'm so nice to them. It's not often they get to meet a fine lady like me.'

Mother was full of contradictions. She admired rich people and the few she knew she'd describe as constituting 'a lovely family', or they were 'fine people', as if material success and moral superiority naturally coincided. She didn't pursue the rich, however, occasionally dismissing them as 'spoiled' and 'idle', especially non-working wives. She admired scientists and doctors most of all, since they contributed to the advancement of humanity. Research was the highest good and Mother would have ranked a poor medical researcher over a rich real estate agent, but she was not given to setting up such clarifying contrasts in her mind. She didn't torment herself over moral quandaries; for her, everything coexisted in a general beige haze.

Not that she couldn't come down hard on cheating or stealing or cursing ('I don't like ugly talk,' she'd say). Nor did she approve of

Edmund White

criticizing other people ('When did you become so high and mighty?'
she'd ask my sister, who had a nasty satirical streak). Mother was more
likely to pity people than ridicule them. Although she believed in
medicine and eventually worked in a free medical clinic for the
retarded and brain damaged at Cook County Hospital in Chicago,
nevertheless, in her inconsistent way, she continued all her life to read
Mary Baker Eddy's texts as well as a magazine published by the
Christian Scientists. What she liked about the Scientists was their uplift,
especially their certitude that evil was only a form of ignorance that
could be banished by wisdom. Mother described herself as 'bouncy'.
The Ford she owned when I was an infant she named Bouncer. She
longed to go on the Arthur Godfrey show as a good-time gal who
was also a mysterious femme fatale. She thought her name, Delilah,
was so alluring that it made her a natural for a talk show.

   She also read Emerson, not for his uncomfortable questions but
for his reassuring answers. She liked his Yankee individuality, joined
to German idealism and Hindu passivity, though she was not one
to ferret out the contradictory sources of his thinking. She was a
pantheist. She liked to believe we were all waves in a single big sea,
that for a moment we rose as individuals before we crashed and were
reabsorbed into the swelling mass. Sometimes we were all mirrors
reflecting the sun, just slightly different glimpses of the same
Oversoul. Even at an early age I found Mother's pantheism attractive
but unconvincing. I never liked God in any form, even at his most
universal. To me he was like Santa Claus—a grown-up conspiracy
perpetrated on children to humiliate them. Too good to be true. Was
I unconvinced by God because he was a man, an adult, white,
authoritative male, and his son seemed an unfamiliar type to me back
then in the 1940s and 1950s: bearded, long-haired, liquid-eyed,
compassionate to the point of morbidity? Mother loved the Christ
of the Sermon on the Mount but her God she took in two
incompatible forms—diffused through nature and concentrated in
one kindly, attentive, all-forgiving grandfather. Christ himself she
thought of as a wise man, nothing more, the Emerson of his day.
Certainly not as God. She rejected Jesus the personal saviour whom
her niece (Jack's daughter) embraced so fervently. After Mother died,
I surmised that her niece believed she was writhing in hell; all
Mother's good works, her daily prayers to God, counted for nothing

since she'd not been born again, she'd not been washed in the blood of the Lamb.

As I was growing up, Mother and I would go on long car trips. After we started living in Evanston outside Chicago we'd drive down to Texas in two or three long days. My sister must have been in the back seat but I can't remember her. Along the way Mother liked me to read to her, hopeful, deep books that would sometimes cause her to look dreamy ('Read that again—we must remember that') or that would make her drum her hands with glee on the steering wheel and bounce up and down with the sheer excitement of absorbing beautiful words and inspiring ideas. Sometimes she'd forgo Emerson and Eddy in favour of something meaty like Bruno Bettelheim's thoughts about death camp survivors or childhood schizophrenia.

For everything she did was oriented to her career. Her reading (or rather her listening, since she'd decided that audition was her natural 'modality' and she was more an aural than a visual learner) gave her ideas or strength for her work, and often I would read aloud articles about retardation from a professional journal. Even her inspirational reading was destined to give her the fortitude and compassion necessary for her draining work.

She had no hobbies, though she could sew and cook. She never minded sewing a button back on or taking tiny neat stitches to repair a tear and I can still see her sitting on the couch, her short legs dangling, her reading glasses weirdly enlarging my view of her eyes, as she performed the humble task with admirable calm and efficiency, often still wearing her fancy work clothes instead of her nightgown. She'd stop everything, wherever she was, and do the bit of sewing required. She would never have wasted her time gardening or playing the piano—or playing cards or even going for a walk. She collected nothing for herself though she bought me a music box for every birthday, all 'improving' in that they played a Chopin waltz or something from Gounod's *Faust*. Everyone she spoke to during the day was a patient or parent, colleague or volunteer, or some sort of 'professional contact'. She worked a full day—at first in the schools, later in her Chicago clinic—and often filled up her evenings doing private testing and consultations.

She had no interest in therapy or purely psychological problems. For her, all mental torment was ultimately due to chemical imbalance, genetic deficits or brain traumas, usually sustained during birth. Her own suffering alone was due to genuine distress, usually caused by men's cruelty. For all the rest of us, she was convinced that birth was so hard on the infant that he or she invariably sustained some form of brain damage. To Mother, everyone alive was brain damaged, a condition obvious if important functions had been disturbed such as speech or hand-eye coordination, less apparent if a subtler form of agnosia had been triggered (the interpretation of visual signals, for instance). When I had trouble learning to drive from a brusque, untalkative instructor who would demonstrate the right moves but never describe them, Mother assured me I would make progress only if I'd switch to a college student who'd talk me through everything and show me nothing. She was right. My birth, apparently, was so long and difficult that her obstetrician had made her promise she would have no more babies. I had several convulsions in my first few weeks. 'He told me to close the store,' she said, laughing one of her laughs, a low, vulgar, humourless, even menacing, chuckle. It strikes me only now that her decision to close the store was timed with (and may have caused) the beginning of Daddy's affair with Kay.

If my sister or I ever spoke of general apathy, a broken heart, listlessness, anxiety, Mother would say, 'I think we should run an electroencephalogram on you,' or 'Maybe you need a good neurological work-up. After all, you had those convulsions...' Quite rightly, she saw deviance and neurosis as an unsoundable swamp and preferred a diagnosis of previously undetected petit mal seizures to one of philosophical despair or psychogenic angst.

She was a hard worker: up at six, at the clinic by seven-thirty, not home till seven or eight, at which time she often saw private cases, as she also did on the weekends. She loved the once-a-week open clinic every Wednesday morning at the hospital when doctors of all different specialties would pool their expertise; she would take notes and write up the final report. She'd describe pitiful, grotesque children as 'a beautiful case of hydrocephalia' or 'a classic example of Down's syndrome'. She'd refer to sickle-cell anaemia or phenylketonuria. As a Southerner she was convinced she could communicate more effectively with blacks than could the Yankee (or Indian or Chinese) doctors. If the doctor would ask if the child 'drooled', Delilah would translate: 'Mother, does your baby pule?'

The Merry Widow

L ike my father, who bragged that he'd never gone bankrupt or killed a man, my mother would also stress the basics. They were children of the frontier. She admired someone like her own mother, who rose early, made her bed, cleaned her house and cooked at least one hot meal a day for herself and Mr Snider. 'When I'm alone in the house,' Mother would say, 'I set myself a place and even put a flower in a bud vase.'

She and Willie Lulu wrote each other one-page letters every day. Sometimes just two or three sentences scrawled in pencil: 'Hot here in the nineties. Need a good rain. Mr Snider still got his summer cold.' Sometimes Grandma would add, ungrammatically, 'Tell Eddie never to smoke nor drank.'

My mother wanted to give me the blanket approval that Willie Lulu had bestowed on her. But Willie had led such a circumscribed life, seldom travelling out of Texas or even Ranger, that she never doubted for a moment what she thought about something. Either it was a part of her familiar, over-observed world, or it was utterly foreign and she said, 'Well, I declare, will wonders never cease,' and she conceded it was beyond her intellectual means.

But Lila Mae had taken on whole new worlds for which she'd not been prepared. Not just the miracles of technology (men walking on the moon)—for those innovations were precisely the ones she could take in her stride since she had been programmed to believe in progress. No, what made her uncertain were the proper boundaries between children and adults, love and sex, work and play. And what bewildered her were her children—their strange, mocking sense of humour, their self-hatred, their duplicity or at least doubleness. Mother couldn't tolerate or even fathom our inexplicable suffering. 'I don't see what you're complaining about,' she'd say. 'You're not deformed, you're well housed and well fed, you attend good schools, your health is excellent, you're both intelligent, in the top percentile of the population, you're of normal height and average weight, you're good-looking kids, you weren't born in Armenia or Mongolia but in the greatest country on earth in a century of splendid medical care— ' She'd look offended and tired when Margaret and I laughed at her chirpiness. My sister didn't like me much (I was too obviously an egghead and nerd and pansy) but as teenagers we did share a bitter sense of humour. Our mother's kind of *statistical* reassurance struck

us as grotesque since we didn't want to be of average weight or
normal height—we wanted to be exceptionally beautiful and lovable.
Whereas in fact we were each obsessed by our own flaws. I knew
that I had a huge black mole growing between my shoulder blades,
that I threw a ball like a faggot, that my big black glasses made me
look like a creep. Margaret hated her teeth, which had gaps between
them because our mother had been too cheap to pay for braces. She'd
rather buy herself a mink coat and a matching mink hat—'I *need* it,'
she'd wail. 'A good appearance is half of professional success. And
I get cold in the winter going down to that ugly old Cook County
Hospital when it's still dark outside in sub-zero weather. I'm with
welfare mothers all day long and babies who are no more than
monsters and I need a bit of luxury in my life. Your teeth look fine,
Margaret Anne. It's all just your imagination. Why can't you
accentuate the positive the way I do?'

But Mother, too, had something she was ashamed of: fat. The
ninety pounds she'd once weighed still seemed to her her rightful,
God-given size. That she now weighed seventy pounds more struck
her as a horrible but temporary aberration. I had no sympathy for
her; being overweight seemed to me to be a form of adult carelessness,
even moral failure. She was always wrestling with her size.

Her girdle was a medieval device called the Merry Widow that
simultaneously cinched in her waist (and made it hard for her to
breathe) and pushed up her breasts with half cups that barely came
up to the nipples. The Widow moulded her ass into one seamless,
rounded sphere, a mono-ass in which no crack was detectable under
her skirt. The girdle, which was French, was laced up the back. That
was my job. First I'd thread the laces around the outer, easier vertical
line of grommets. Once they were in place Mother would inhale
deeply and suck in her stomach, and like a professional torturer I'd
shift the laces to the inner line of grommets, one by one. She would
groan from the pain but stoically order me to go on pulling them
as tight as I could. Her hair was wild, as brittle and blown-up as a
tumbleweed from years and years of sitting under the dryer, her pale
face not yet made up, featureless and shiny, her height minuscule
since she wasn't wearing her high heels, to which she'd become so
habituated that her calf muscles had shrunk and now she couldn't
walk more than a few paces without stretching them painfully. Once

she was strapped into the Merry Widow she could clip her nylons in place, apply her make-up, brush and spray her hair into shape, slip on her dress (which I'd have to zip up), put on her woven white-and-yellow-gold bracelet and matching brooch and her black oval ring with the carved intaglio of Athena's head in profile, finally step into her immaculately polished high heels and douse herself with perfume, grab a purse that matched her shoes and shrug into the three-quarter-length mink cape she'd had her full-length coat reduced to on the theory that people would think she'd been able to afford a new fur at the newly fashionable length.

There was no provision for wearing panties under the girdle. Maybe some women did but Mother would have been too obese to bend over and pull them down to urinate, which she had to do frequently during the day. Because she was pantyless her black bush was visible just below the bottom of her girdle when she was not wearing a dress. Margaret thought this situation repulsive and unhygienic and wouldn't help Mother into her foundation garment. 'Oh, God,' she'd moan to me, 'it's *so* yucky. Somebody could look up her skirt and see *everything*, and she wears that damn girdle every day—it's not even clean! Most women wear big baggy panties over the girdle—why can't she? Is she a pervert?' Although even young slender women were expected to wear girdles under fitted suits and evening dresses, Margaret categorically refused. She'd been plump as a ten- and eleven-year-old, but as a teen she'd become lean and athletic and she knew she didn't have to compress her hips and stomach into a rubberized tube. When I was a high school freshman I slow-danced at a school party with a famous local beauty. Under the chiffon I could feel the unyielding bones and webbing of the girdle. Girls were revealing their bare shoulders and arms to admiring men, but mothers made sure their daughters' bodies, the important parts at least, were armoured inside strong, protective foundations.

The minute our mother would come home she'd say, 'Get me out of this girdle!' She'd throw off her dress and I would unlace her as quickly as possible, keeping my eyes away from the glossy bush below. Her extremely white skin was inflamed and waffled as it emerged out of the Widow. Mother visibly sagged into a bigger, rounder, shorter shape. She'd throw on her nightgown even if it was only five in the evening. She used cold cream to remove her elaborate make-up. She believed that a woman should never wash her face. In fact, water must never touch the skin. No, she must thoroughly slather it in cold cream then wipe it off with cotton balls. To this daily ritual she attributed her glowing, unwrinkled complexion—a claim she'd make loudly and clearly to anyone present, despite the incontrovertible evidence that her face was covered with a mass of tiny wrinkles around her mouth and eyes and two deep creases across her forehead.

Once her face was stripped of paint she'd make herself her first highball of the evening. 'Ooh-eeh, I need a drink, brother!' she'd say, the barnyard exclamation an echo of her mother, though Willie had never sipped a drink in her life. Mother diluted her inch of scotch with a tall glassful of water and ice; she kept a highball going throughout the evening. She'd write up reports in her neat, round hand, which her secretary at the clinic would type the next day. She didn't approve of television though she liked it ('I don't see how you can watch that dumb stuff') just as she enjoyed popular music but usually only let herself listen to Mozart's 'Jupiter' symphony or Beethoven's 'Moonlight' sonata. 'I like fine music,' she'd say, 'beautiful, deep music meant for the ages.' I would laugh at her cruelly, mockingly, though I agreed with her completely.

Somewhere along the line my sister and I had decided our mother was a character, a caricature like Tennessee Williams's Blanche DuBois or Amanda Wingfield. Lila Mae's baseless optimism, her coquetry, her insistence that she was 'an old-fashioned gal' and 'one hundred per cent feminine' made us grin like gargoyles. Adolescents are wretchedly conventional as they tiptoe nervously into the great crowded ballroom of adulthood. Margaret and I were ashamed that our mother was a divorcee—a 'gay divorcee' as she put it, to our minds as dubious as a 'Merry Widow'. In Evanston in the 1950s, during the Eisenhower years, a divorcee was just a step away from a prostitute. Our mother said she left Cincinnati because she needed 'a big stage, a big world, I need to think big and be with big people who have big ideas.' But if she'd stayed put she would have been humiliated every day since there were no single men or women in their world in Cincinnati and all the couples they had known would have sided—*did* side!—with Daddy and Kay. A divorcee was seen as a potential husband stealer and home wrecker.

When we lived in Dallas Mother was not allowed to sit at the bar or dine alone in the restaurant at the Baker hotel: no unaccompanied women was their policy. When we moved back to Illinois, Mother made up for lost time. She became a habitué of Chicago's supper clubs and piano bars. Her favourite place was Ricardo's, an Italian restaurant and bar in the Rush Street area of nightclubs near the Chicago River down behind the Wrigley Building. The lighting was low, the creamy pasta dishes comforting, the waiters friendly. Mrs White was a good tipper and a real lady (she'd tell you so herself). Short and fat and girdled, smiling and drunk and fearless, Delilah would clamber with some difficulty up on a stool and eat her noodles Alfredo at the demilune bar behind which were illuminated full-length paintings of the vices and virtues, abstractions that struck a Christian Scientist as theatrical and unreal. I can remember one naked man transfixed in a pitiless shaft of light. Another canvas by Ivan Albright, Chicago's best-known artist, showed a hag covered with sores and cellulite; we were told that Albright had worked on it for ten years. I also recall a scaly, infected-looking painting by him with a long portentous title; it was no accident that Albright had painted the picture of Dorian Gray for the movie, both the bland Before and the oozing, scary After.

When I accompanied my mother to Ricardo's we'd be seated at a corner table within hailing distance of the bar. We never had enough money to order without thinking; Mother would split a green salad with me and then split a pasta dish. She claimed she ate like a bird and probably most of her calories did come from whisky. An accordionist—always the same little, deferential man—would come by our table and serenade us, his mouth producing a sad smile and his head cocked to one side.

One evening at our corner table, where Mother always kept the highballs coming, she turned her unfocused smile on the extremely tall businessman at the bar who kept glancing over. 'Roberto,' she whispered to her favourite waiter, 'do you know anything about that very tall man—don't look now!—that tall man at the bar?'

'Oh, that's Abe, Mrs White. I don't know his last name, big tipper, owns a yacht that he keeps down on the marina here. Lives somewhere nearby on the Gold Coast, I think he said.'

'That's interesting,' Mother said with a smile. 'That's *very* interesting.'

Maybe Abe noticed them conferring about him, because Roberto came over a moment later with a new highball and a ginger ale for me. 'Compliments of Abe,' he whispered. Rather than exclaiming with excitement as I would have predicted, Mother merely smiled with boozy serenity and raised her glass to toast Abe, her head tilted slightly to one side. Her smile was pursed as if to reproach him tenderly for an extravagance. A minute later he was standing at our table.

'May I join you?' he asked.

Mother smiled enigmatically and nodded and he slipped into the booth beside her and reached over to shake my hand. 'Abe Silverstein,' he said. It all seemed so easy to me and I wondered if Mother was sober enough not to ruin this chance. For it did appear a remarkable opportunity since I knew that Mother sat beside the silent phone night after night, anxious and depressed, because none of the men she'd given her number to at Ricardo's or at the Miller Steak House ever called her. At age fourteen I had replicated within myself all of her doubts about herself—was she too old, too fat, too short, too drunk to attract this tall slender man in his forties with the unseasonable tan and the shiny dome circled by a monk's tonsure of dark curls, with the well tailored suit that gave him staggeringly wide shoulders and exposed an elegant quarter inch of white shirt cuffs, this man with the bright smile and the one winningly chipped tooth, with the big warm dry hand (I could imagine his hands trying to unlace the complicated genetic code of the Merry Widow's double helix)? I felt anxiety building up inside of me. Should I say something remarkable that would win Abe over? That would lure him into a relationship with Mother, with us?

Mother spoke too much about herself, about her work with the retarded, and I squirmed with irritation at her ineptness. Didn't she know that men needed to be drawn out, made to feel important? 'I love my work,' she said, 'because I feel I'm making a real contribution to retardation.' She's retarded herself, I thought.

But Abe wasn't put off. 'That's just great, Delilah,' he said. 'I didn't think I'd be meeting someone classy like you in a place like this.'

'Like me?' Mother asked disingenuously. 'Whatever do you mean?'

She wanted him to elaborate on how unexpectedly important and admirable she was, but he didn't pick up on his cue and instead started rambling on about other interesting men and women he'd

Lila Mae at the opening for 'Little City', a charity for disabled children that she helped to found in Chicago, c.1960

Edmund White

met at Ricardo's. Naturally, Mother didn't want to hear about them. She didn't want to be placed in a context, no matter how flattering. She wanted to hear that she was unique. Her smile faded from the goodwill she'd radiated when she'd been talking about herself into a drunken fragment of resentment and impatience. If I'd been in her pumps I would have produced all the appropriate little nods and murmurs of assent, but she went inert and heavy with frustration. I'd learned to make myself extremely agreeable to the two or three handsome guys my age I knew at Evanston High (in a year I'd be sent off to prep school). I admitted they'd never sleep with me but I wanted them to enjoy themselves so much in my company that they'd gravitate to me almost unconsciously. Mother had perfected none of my dark arts.

She could always fall back on Mr Hamilton, a newspaperman who liked nothing more than to have Mother prepare him a hot buttery meal. Then they'd watch a variety show on television. He was half blind and couldn't drive, which removed any reason for his going easy on the bourbons and branch water. He had been in the newspaper business for nearly forty years but he exhibited no interest in current events or office gossip and relayed no anecdotes of interest. I think he made up the pages, chose which stories would run where and for how many inches. His conversation was all boilerplate, the odd bits of information used to fill up columns. In some ways he was Mother's version of Mr Snider—a big soft man who was companionable. Mother kept hoping for someone better and when she thought things were working out with Abe she'd dismiss the thought of Mr Hamilton with scorn. 'I need a real man,' she'd say. 'Someone who's got some oomph.'

But when better prospects would vanish she'd go back to preparing homey dinners for Mr Hamilton or let him invite her out for a big, sizzling steak at Miller's and a baked potato engorged with sour cream and chives.

As I grew older I became more and more difficult with my mother just as she was becoming sadder and lonelier. When I turned fifteen she was fifty-three; she was finding fewer and fewer men to ask her out, she was nearly as wide as she was tall and she was constantly out of breath. When I'd let myself in at midnight after a date she'd want to know every detail about my evening. She'd be

58

lying awake in bed in her darkened room just beside the front hallway. I knew she couldn't sleep until I came home and I resented this form of emotional blackmail. Nor did she suffer in silence. 'Remember,' she'd say, 'I won't be able to sleep a wink until you're safely back here, and I've got a killing schedule at the clinic tomorrow. Please don't keep me up all night, honey.'

When I'd stand in her doorway at midnight she'd want me to sit on the edge of her bed and rub her back; sometimes she'd turn on a light and ask me to press out the blackheads. Her skin felt clammy. I could smell the whisky seeping from her pores; in a kittenish way she called it 'wicky'.

'Was she cute, that Helen of yours?' she'd ask.

I felt trapped, compromised by her nosiness, revolted by the touch of her skin which, however, was terribly familiar. I didn't want to discuss girls with her. I had bought a latch for my bedroom door and installed it myself so I'd have a little privacy, but she was always tapping at the door. If I didn't respond she'd say, 'Now Eddie, you either open this door for your mother or I'm going to break it down.' And I knew she would and could. If I stayed in the bath too long she'd shout through the locked door, 'You've washed it long enough.'

As a little boy I'd lived for her. I'd suffered when she wept over the divorce (which we referred to as the 'XA', a term I'd made up out of a superstitious fear of naming it). I had read to her the beautiful words of Emerson and felt the same glow of admiration as she did, for such depth, such wisdom. I would sometimes cry hysterically when I was unable to console her. In my fantasies (and in my responses to the ink-blot tests she was administering to me) I saw empty royal palaces and objects—jewels and graveyards—just as when I built castles of sand in the summer or of snow in the winter I peopled them with lonely, tragic tsarinas floating through crumbling wings of the Old Palace that had long since been abandoned.

But as I grew older I resented my mother's dependence.

When she'd say, 'You and I are exactly alike,' I would reply, 'Oh no we're not. You like to lump everything together. You prefer resemblance to difference—that's why you like the Baha'i Temple in Glencoe, because they claim all the nine great religions of the world are *really* the same. But they're not! You have to make distinctions and not lump things together. That's your biggest mistake.'

Edmund White

Her 'mistakes' were legion to my eyes. She was unafraid of the
obvious. I lorded over her my more extensive reading, my better
memory, my more critical approach to life, forgetting that if I had
respect for the mind it was due to her. I attacked her for not keeping
her distance, for not respecting my autonomy; I could make her cry
but if I was nice to her, even for a moment, she'd be all smiles and
forgive my trespasses against her. I felt she loved me without
understanding me, just as her mother loved us all but knew little
about us. Mother saw me as a sort of philosopher king, something
like her secular vision of Christ. In her view, I was eager to make
my 'contribution' in order to reduce the sum total of human
suffering. When she finally accepted that I was a gay writer, she'd
say, 'You've truly become a spokesman for your people.' Gays were
my tribe and I was leading them into the Promised Land. I knew I
was selfish and egotistical and too afraid of failure, obscurity and
poverty to be able to afford the luxury of 'helping my people'.

In the late 1970s, when I was approaching forty and she seventy,
she was drinking so much that she could scarcely walk to the corner.
Her belly was a swollen watermelon under her girdle, her face
resembled that of a squalling infant—creased, nearly toothless, red.
She'd been forced into retirement when the clinic she headed at Cook
County Hospital closed its doors. It had been a private clinic, if in a
public hospital, and it had been financed by rich Jewish benefactors,
friends of Abraham Levinson, the doctor who'd established the
foundation after his son's early death and named it in his honour.
Now Dr Levinson was dead, too, as were most of his friends. Whereas
the clinic (and my mother) had been pioneers in the diagnosis and
treatment of retarded and brain damaged children, now, thirty years
later, better care had become common and there was no need for the
Julius D. Levinson Foundation. My mother was forced into retirement
with no pension and no savings; she had nothing but the pitiful
monthly sums she received from Social Security.

And the money I gave her. I sent her a cheque every month for
the next twenty years; in that way I had replaced my father, who
was now dead, and his alimony, which had run out. I maintained
my mother in her fancy Gold Coast apartment with its doorman and
view of Lake Michigan. I paid her dress bills at Neiman's and Saks
Fifth Avenue. Actually, she economized so skilfully—she who had

always been recklessly extravagant—that she was able to afford her little luxuries even on the small sums I was able to spare.

At the same time as my mother lost her job she had a second mastectomy. Her latest and much younger boyfriend found a job in California, took his leave and was never heard from again. He'd been a self-serving drip, but Mother had loved him and losing him was a terrible blow for her. Mother felt he couldn't endure the loss of her second breast (not to mention her colostomy, for altogether she suffered from three primary cancers, poor battered thing). As if these trials had not been harsh enough, she couldn't keep up the payments on her modest summer house and had to sell it. Jobless, loveless, breastless and homeless, she began drinking so heavily that one night, driving home to the house she was about to vacate, she crashed into the garage door then staggered inside and fell in the bathroom. She cracked a rib and was unable to get up. No one knew she was there and no one came looking for her. One day went by, then a second. By now thoroughly sober but in terrible pain and still immobilized, she began to worry about a new complication. She was too weak to irrigate her colostomy and her peristalsis seemed to have shut down. She knew that soon she'd be poisoned by her backed-up faeces.

It was then she made her strange bargain with God. She told him that if he'd unplug her colostomy she'd never touch another drink. No sooner had she made this deal with the deity than the shit began to shoot out of her side. And she honoured her promise of abstinence ever after.

Once she stopped drinking she succumbed to the most terrible delusions. My sister and I failed to see that she had the DTs though her symptoms were classic. She boarded a plane for Amarillo where she descended on her brother Jack's daughter. Two days later my cousin was on the phone: 'Eddie, you've got to come down here and get Aunt Lila Mae. She's gone crazy. You know those little bugs we have down here we call millers? Well, there were just three or four millers flying around the ceiling light last night but your mother saw *thousands*, revolving like devils at the mouth of hell. Now you know, Eddie, I keep a nice clean house, a Christian house. Your poor mother is out of control. I don't know anything about her business, but I kind of suspect she's not a rich, rich woman...?'

'Not at all,' I said.

Edmund White

'Well, she's offering money, even very large sums, to just about everyone she meets. She's not at all nasty. She's as sweet as sweet can be. But she never draws a breath; I hear her in her room talking to herself, very excited and bubbly, like a little girl. You know I've always thought Aunt Lila Mae is a very special person. I love her to bits. She's believed in me all my life when my own mother did nothing but criticize me and tear me down. I owe your mother so much but I just don't know what to do now.'

I flew down to Amarillo and Mother was at the airport in a funny little costume she'd cobbled together, with pompoms in her hands. She'd decided she was a cheerleader. Her eyes wouldn't meet mine, her smile was a manic blur and she was singing a little pep song of her own devising: 'Go, Eddie, go, go, go.'

At this time my sister and I grew closer as it dawned on us that we were no longer neglected children but newly needed if not officially designated guardians to our mother. She had been too unhappy, too obsessed with her work and men, too alcoholic to be the serene, all-giving, nothing-taking goddess for whom our society reserves the label 'Good Mother'. But she'd given herself to us entirely, we were the brats who rattled behind her like cans tied to a cat's tail and we were the excess baggage who'd prevented any man from ever proposing to her after the divorce, or so she firmly believed.

Although she'd rocked us and hugged us and wept as she did so when we were small, later my sister and I wouldn't let her touch us. We were repelled by her body—so fat, so corseted; I am certain this distaste was inspired by her own self-loathing and her drunken, coquettish demands for massages.

I have replicated too many of her traits to be entitled to judge her. I alternate thin decades with fat decades; the thin periods have always been hard-won through medically supervised dieting, exercise and even surgery. Like her I am always pursuing one man or another, though unlike her I've usually lived with my lovers for an average of five years at a time. Recently when a lover left me, I sobbed for two months just as my mother had when one of her boyfriends left her. Like her I'm work-obsessed, but I've certainly never put in the long, hard days she relished and bemoaned. Like her I've had my problems with alcohol and had to stop drinking altogether. Like her I alternate between low self-esteem and a prickly sense of my own importance.

Eventually my mother straightened herself out. As her DTs subsided she hid out in a Michigan hotel, scribbling away at her memoirs, just as I'm doing now. She discovered the only effective cure for mental illness: room service. She was able to summon another living human being—a handsome young waiter—whenever she wanted him. And since she was in small-town mid-America she could engage him in conversation as long as she liked. Whenever she felt threatened by his presence she could dismiss him with a smile and a large tip. Whenever he appeared he brought her warm, nourishing food. No hospital or clinic or doctor can provide this precise winning formula.

My father's death left my mother nonplussed. In her own mind she'd been involved year after year in the most dramatic communication with him, a dialogue constructed out of silent replies, some silences short, others heavy with irony or protest, still others staccato and excited and overlapping. Now all that artful combative silence had ended, replaced by the senseless low telephone buzz of death. What she'd always believed to be a heavily meaningful rupture in communication she now understood had long since gone dead for him and perhaps had never been interesting enough for him to notice. He didn't give a damn about her, never had.

She was so incapable of grasping that her long years of work as a psychologist were over that she rented a one-room office at the top of her building—the 'crow's nest', as she called it—and filled it with metal filing cabinets containing hundreds and hundreds of case histories. These were documents. They were official. They must be preserved. She might be held accountable, possibly before the law. She might be called on as an expert witness.

She teamed up with her grandson Keith, my sister's son. He and his mother were on the outs for the moment so his grandmother moved him into the crow's nest—which gave her a graceful excuse for no longer going up to her desk and files and staring dumbly at the yellowing folders and the names of retarded children who were now forty or fifty years old if still alive. My nephew was her new project. Mother would make him supper and then he'd read to her out loud, no longer from Bruno Bettelheim's but from my books. Yes, I'd replaced Mary Baker Eddy and all those wise men; no matter that my pages were too ironic to read comfortably, too descriptive and dirty to be uplifting. In a different way my nephew had replaced me, the young male person who could stimulate Delilah's reveries, plunge her into a serene ecstasy; no matter that he wasn't a worshipful seven-year-old sissy but, rather, an unhappy young adult who was laughing at his cracked granny half the time. She could thicken her skin wilfully to signs of mockery so long as she could obtain a rough simulacrum of her old familiar rituals.

She'd turn down the lights and listen to Pavarotti singing Puccini. My nephew liked Bach or Morrissey but sentimental Italian warbling wasn't his demitasse of espresso. Yet he was tolerant. And how hard was it, to listen to his old granny praising his 'genius' (as a writer, as a guitarist and songwriter, as a student of literature)? She was certain that he, too, would make an important contribution, as his grandmother had done, working with the retarded, as his mother was doing as a social worker and therapist, as his Uncle Eddie was doing liberating his homosexual tribe. She beamed with joy at the swooning beauty of 'Nessun dorma' and drummed her tiny fists against the invisible gong suspended just before her in the air— gleaming, the metal mottled, the surface immense.   □

GRANTA

THE GRIEF OF
STRANGERS
Chimamanda Ngozi Adichie

Chinechelum said little as her mother drove her to the airport. She looked out of the window, at the trees whose leaves had turned the colour of a ripe banana, or a berry-red, and others that had shed all their leaves and stood with their naked branches sticking up. It was one of the things she liked to talk about: fall in New England, how it looked like the flowers had lent their colours to the leaves. She liked to talk about summer, too, how the sun lingered and flirted until late. Or winter, how there was something primal about the stillness of snow and the cold needles at the tips of her ears. 'Please,' her mother would say. 'Please, *nne*, try and talk about something real.' Her mother said it always in that pleading-pitying tone, as if to say she knew Chinechelum had to be handled with care but it still had to be said. Before they left for the airport that morning, her mother had said in that same tone, 'When you get to London, *biko*, try and talk normally to Odin.' And she had wanted to tell her mother that she *had* talked to Odin on the phone, hadn't she? Odin had seemed to find her conversation normal enough, too, because he had invited her to visit, hadn't he? But she said, 'Mama, I will.'

She would try and talk normally, although she was not sure what normally was. Was it the self-indulgence people lapped up from one another these days, the mutual navel-gazing that went on at the recent faculty holiday party, for example? She had listened to a string of self-reflexives, the things that the 'I' would do or had done or wished to do with, or to, the 'me.' Nobody talked about things outside of themselves, and if they did, it became about the relationship of those things to the 'me' or the 'I'. But maybe it was the way conversation had always been. Maybe she had been away from life for too long and she didn't recognize the rules any more. Nine years was a long time. That holiday party was her first party, indeed her first social function, in so long. And maybe it was what had finally made her give in to the idea of her mother and Aunty Ngolika 'connecting' her to a husband, a Nigerian man. *Connect.* That word had amused her, still amused her now.

She rolled the window down a little because the car heater was turned on high, and recalled the first few Nigerian men she'd been 'connected' to, whom she had talked to on the phone, who had faked American accents and littered their conversation with clunky mentions of BMWs and suburban houses. But Odin had been different, perhaps because he had said little about himself when they talked, had come across as self-confident without needing anything to prop him up. Or so she thought. It was Aunty Ngolika who found him. 'The only thing is that he does not live in the US, he lives in London,' Aunty Ngolika had said, in an almost conspiratorial whisper. 'But you can easily relocate, it shouldn't be a problem.' Chinechelum had wanted to ask her aunt why the man—she hadn't been told his name was Odin then—could not relocate. But she didn't ask, because she didn't want to come across as the old Chinechelum, the one her mother said was distant and faraway, the one her mother had worried so much about. She wanted to be the new one who was willing to live again.

When they got to the airport, her mother hugged her and held her face between hands that were scrubbed weekly in the Korean-owned nail studio and said, 'I am praying, *nnem*, it will work out.' Chinechelum nodded, looking at her mother's anxious face with its thin-shaved eyebrows. She wished she had her mother's enthusiasm and her mother's serious hope. She wished that she felt something, anything, rather than the numbness that still wrapped itself around her, that had wrapped itself around her for nine years.

Before she boarded her flight, she saw a woman hugging her children and husband. The woman had unsightly jerry-curl hair. Her heavy make-up streaked as she cried. Her children were crying. Her husband was looking away with a false braveness. Chinechelum watched them for a while and then started to cry. She had discovered that she had the uncanny ability to participate in the grief of strangers, and so she felt the acute pain of that family, crying at the airport, at their looming separation.

Chinechelum liked the claustrophobic feel of London, the way everything seemed to be too small, too tight. She liked the tiny room in her cousin Amara's cramped flat and the concrete neighbourhood with no trees and the scarred brick walls of the apartment building. Amara had been talking to her non-stop since they hugged at the Arrivals in Heathrow, and now Amara's nine-year-old son was shouting as he played a video game in front of the TV. Amara's voice, her son's shouting, the sounds from the TV, irritated Chinechelum, made her feel a throbbing tightness at her temples.

'These West Indian women are taking our men and our men are stupid enough to follow them. Next thing, they will have a baby and they don't want the men to marry them oh, they just want child support,' Amara was saying when Jonathan screamed, his eyes now glued to the TV screen.

'Turn down the volume, Jonathan,' Amara said.

'Mum!'

'Turn down the volume right now!'

'Mum! I can't hear!'

He didn't turn down the volume and Amara didn't say anything else to him; instead she turned to Chinechelum to continue talking.

'You know,' Chinechelum said, wrapping her arms around herself, 'It's interesting how much we forgive our children because they have foreign accents.'

'What do you mean?'

'Back home in Nigeria, Jonathan would be punished.'

Amara looked away. 'I'm going to take that game away from him soon oh.'

But Chinechelum knew she would not, because Jonathan was her son from her broken marriage and his father was rich and he came back from his weekends at his father's house with new toys and the least Amara imagined she could do to maintain her son's respect was to let him do whatever he wanted.

Amara was talking again. 'I met this man recently. He is kind oh, but he is so bush. He grew up in Onitsha and so you can imagine what kind of bush accent he has. He mixes up *ch* and *sh*. I want to go to the *ch*opping centre. Sit down on a *sh*eer. Anyway, he told me he was willing to marry me and adopt Jonathan. Willing! As if he was doing charity work. Willing! Imagine that. But it's not his fault, it's because we are in London, after all, and water never finds its different levels here. He is the kind of man I would never even look at in Nigeria, not to talk of going out with. But you know London is a leveller.'

Chinechelum thought about what Amara had just said—London is a leveller. It amused her. It amused her the way Nigerians in the diaspora complained that the class lines blurred outside Nigeria, that upstarts rose to take places that they would never even dream about in Nigeria. London is a leveller.

'Are you all right, Chelum?' Amara asked. 'You look distant.'

Chinechelum stretched out her legs, still hugging herself. She and Amara had grown up together in Enugu, shared dolls as children, gone to Queens' College Lagos and graduated the same year, before the coup happened and Amara's family moved to England and her own family moved to the United States. Now, she watched Amara, thirty-eight with bleached brownish-yellow hair and vermilion coloured talons. 'Are *you* okay, Amara?' she asked mildly. 'You look like a bad fake of some sort of doll.'

The minute she said it, she wished she hadn't, because it was very much like the old Chinechelum, the one who her mother said had forgotten the delicate rules of living. But Amara did not look offended. And Chinechelum knew that it was because Amara—her whole extended family in fact—had devised a means of dealing with her, a strategy she liked to call Containment. She thought of a letter her mother had once written to the whole family; it had been written nine years ago but she had read it again recently, the weekend she visited her mother and started to go through her mother's drawers. Her mother had kept a copy; she was a meticulous record keeper. *Chinechelum has not been herself since Ikeadi's tragedy*, her mother's loopy handwriting said. *Don't take anything she tells you personal. Don't react to anything. She will get over it with time but she will need our patience.*

Now, she wondered if Amara was thinking about that letter and choosing not to be offended. Amara had always been incredibly even-tempered, anyway. Too-nice, some had said she was, when they were in secondary school. And perhaps that too-nice person still existed underneath the angst of the Divorced and Unsatisfied and Almost-forty.

'I'm sorry, Amara,' Chinechelum said. 'I didn't mean it like that.'

'It's all right,' Amara said, adding after a pause, 'So what of Ikeadi? Have there been any changes? I mean, will he never, well, be normal again?'

'Who's to say? Chinechelum replied. 'Miracles happen, don't they? So who's to say?'

'Those goats,' Amara muttered. But Chinechelum knew that Amara was saying that for her, because Amara imagined it was what she wanted to hear. What had happened to Ikeadi was too long ago for Amara, too long for everyone but her. The collective anger of her family and friends had become diluted with time, even though none of them would ever admit it. And now in Amara's eyes she saw that pity that was reserved for people who were not even aware that they deserved pity.

'I think I'll go out for a while,' she said. 'I'll get a day's travelcard and explore.'

Amara looked doubtful. 'Do you want me to come with you? Will you be okay?'

'I'll be fine.'

'Will you do some shopping? Do you have something to wear to your date with Odin?'

'I didn't realize I had to shop for something to wear.'

'Oh, but Chelum, you used to like shopping. You used to walk around all over the centre of London and in the end you would tell me everything was cheaper in the outlet malls in America and you would buy from there instead,' Amara said, and the wistfulness in her voice, in her eyes, amused Chinechelum. She used to like bargain shopping, in her old life with Ikeadi, used to know all the outlet malls in the tri-state area, even befriended the managers so they called her when there was a sale. Her taste had reflected Ikeadi, too: sometimes she'd searched for hours for discounted shirts that made a political statement but had a designer label. Still, she felt no nostalgia for that life, even now that she was walking towards living again.

A blue-grey dusk was settling over London when Chinechelum walked into the Starbucks near Embankment tube station and sat down to a mocha and a blueberry muffin. The soles of her feet ached pleasantly. It was not very cold here—nothing compared to chilly Connecticut for sure—and she had been sweating in her wool pea coat which now hung on the back of her chair. Somebody had left a *New Statesman* on the table and she started to read it. She felt comfortable, cosy even, and was warming quickly to an article about Byron in the books section when a Pakistani woman and a little boy came up to ask if they could share her table. She did not realize how quickly the cafe had filled up.

'Of course,' she said, and shifted her bag, even though it had not been on the side of the table that they would use.

The woman was wearing a nose ring, a tiny glass-like thing that glittered as she moved her head this way and that. Her son looked eight or nine years old, wearing a Mickey Mouse sweater and clutching a blue Gameboy. It took Chinechelum a little while to realize that he was flirting with her. First, he asked if the narrow wooden sticks next to the packets of sugar were for stirring. She said that they were. Then he asked if she had enough room for her magazine—if she wanted him to move his chair. Then he snapped at his mother and said, 'I'm not a baby!' when she wanted to cut his muffin.

He had a delightful chubby face and spoke elegant English with what she assumed to be the accent of the Privileged Pakistani. She imagined a huge house in Karachi, their cars and servants, and his mother with the nose ring struggling to make him grow up responsible and unspoiled amid it all.

'Do you live in London?' he leaned over to ask. And before she could respond, his mother cut in quickly in a smooth language and he glared at her.

'I'm sorry,' his mother said, turning to Chinechelum. 'He talks too much.'

'It's all right,' Chinechelum said. She closed the *New Statesman* to signal that she was open to make conversation.

'His father passed away last year,' his mother whispered. 'This is out first vacation in London without him. We used to do it every year before Christmas.' The woman nodded continuously as she spoke and the boy looked annoyed, as if he had not wanted Chinechelum to know that.

'Oh,' Chinechelum said.

'We went to the Tate,' the boy said.

'Did you like it?' she asked.

He scowled, and she knew he imagined that he looked older doing that. 'It was boring.'

His mother rose. 'We should go. We're going to the theatre later.' She turned to her son and added, 'You're not taking that Gameboy in, you know that.'

The boy ignored her, said 'bye' to Chinechelum, and turned towards the door. Chinechelum knew he wanted to linger, and that it was the reason he had hardly touched his muffin. She watched

them leave. She wished so much that she had asked him his name
and that she had asked his mother a little about her late husband.
A freezing drizzle was falling when she left the cafe. She walked
to the tube station, feeling the tiny raindrops splatter on her coat,
and when she got there, she was absorbed by how many frothy blobs
of spit were on the stairs. She was thinking that there might be a
poem somewhere here—perhaps a free verse, a ramble on the chaos
and spit and style of London—when her train came. Later, she sat
on the stained seat of the noisy train holding the *New Statesman* in
her hand and thought about the Pakistani woman, and the little boy,
and their grief that was so lacquered by activities and muffins and
arguments. Quietly, she started to cry.

Odin was handsome; she knew that already from the photo he'd
sent her as an email attachment. But seeing him, face-to-face,
she saw the cragginess glossed over by the photo finish, and she
thought it made him even more attractive. She didn't know another
man who smiled so much, showing a flash of very white teeth that
she was certain he bleached.

They sat in the dim basement of a French restaurant in Soho, a
glowing candle between them as they both ate a goat's cheese salad.
She had ordered first and then he'd said he would have the same.
She wondered what he would say if she told him that she had not
sat in a restaurant with a man in nine years. Would he consider her
strange, like her Aunty Ngolika had said? 'Don't tell him about
Ikeadi yet, or he might think you a little strange. Wait until you get
close,' Aunty Ngolika had suggested. It had amused Chinechelum
because she hadn't even imagined telling Odin about Ikeadi.

'You're so beautiful,' Odin said. 'I'm surprised some man hasn't
carried you off since.'

She stabbed a piece of lettuce on her plate, slightly alarmed. Were
there no rules to this game? Was marriage alluded to so soon? 'You're
not too bad yourself,' she said. Her mother would like her saying
that. It sounded normal. She'd heard it at the faculty party last year.
The Eighteenth Century Literature woman two offices from hers had
lurched up to the department head and said, 'You are a fucking
amazing writer,' and he replied, 'You're not too bad yourself,' and
everybody around them laughed until they staggered. Chinechelum

Chimamanda Ngozi Adichie

had wondered if it was just their drunkenness, but it seemed not, because Odin was laughing now.

'You're so unusual,' he said. 'You have this look on your face, as if you are detached from everything and yet you're not. It's fascinating.'

She drank some water, not sure what to say.

'So what is it really like living in New England?' Odin asked.

Chinechelum launched into a poetic vignette about New England in the fall, about the blushing sun and nature's different shades of gold and crisp winds chasing carrot-coloured leaves. Odin looked taken aback. Finally he said, 'Mm, that's interesting. You know, whenever I hear New England, I see Connecticut and Maine and places like that and I imagine it's just full of white people.'

'Well, there is some diversity. The student body in my classes is about ten per cent black.' Chinechelum shrugged, and hoped it looked natural. 'The food is very good,' she added, looking down at her plate.

They ate in silence for a while, a silence that she was too aware of. She was too conscious of the movements of the fork in her hand from plate to mouth, of the movements of his jaw.

'So,' he said, putting his fork down. 'How is it going?'

She was not sure what he meant. During one of their telephone conversations, she had mentioned that she had just received a grant and taken a sabbatical to try and complete her book of poetry. Did he mean the poetry? Or did he mean right now, their meal, their meeting? 'How is what going?' she asked.

He laughed. 'I don't know. Just wanted to engage you. You seemed to be faraway.'

'Oh no, I'm here,' she said and sat up straighter.

While they had dessert—they shared a tiramisu—he talked about the attitudes some Nigerian men in the diaspora had about women. They think they can sleep around and it's okay but the woman can't. They sit and watch TV while the woman cooks even though they both work the same hours. He said all of this, shaking his head in a way that meant he thought these men should know better. And she realized, touched, that he was trying to tell her what he was like, or perhaps what he wanted to be like.

He was holding her hand now, both hands clasped on the table.

'I'm so glad we met,' he said. It struck her then that there was something generic about the scene; it could have been any other woman with him, any other educated Nigerian woman, resident abroad, thirty years and above, looking for a man. It didn't have to be her.

Her mother and Aunty Ngolika called two-way, and she listened to two strained voices ask how the dinner had gone, and gasp when she said she wasn't seeing him until Friday. 'Hei! But that's three days away! Was it your suggestion or his?'

It was her suggestion, of course, since Odin had asked her to have lunch with him the next day; in fact he had asked her to come home with him that night.

'It was Odin's idea. He is very busy at work,' she said.

'Mh, that is not a good sign.' She was not sure who had said that, because her mother and aunt sounded alike. Then her mother asked, hesitantly, 'Did you talk normally, *nne?*' And Chinechelum said, calmly, 'Yes, Mama, I did.'

After she hung up, Amara said there was a party in somebody's house in Bayswater, a Yoruba friend, and she thought it would be good for Chinechelum to go.

Chinechelum said she would rather stay at home and read, that she had not finished the *New Statesman*, that the least she could do with a magazine she had not paid for was finish reading it. Amara gave her a long patient look but said nothing. After Amara left, Chinechelum imagined what the party would be like. She had gone to a few with Ikeadi; it didn't matter if they were Christmas or engagement or birthday parties because they were all the same, steeped in jollof rice and jealousy, pepper soup and whispers of who had bought a new flat in Chelsea or a house in suburban Chicago and who had had an autistic baby and whose wife had packed her things and left and who had still not got his legal stay or his green card and who was involved in dirty credit card fraud money and whose husband went back to Nigeria to sleep around with young-young girls. It—the party in Bayswater—was what her mother would consider normal.

Chinechelum ran into Neville Lipton the next day. She had met him before; Amara had introduced them, and later muttered to Chinechelum that the neighbours called him the Overbearing

Oxbridge Octogenarian. But Amara liked him, as did the other neighbours in the block of flats, because he gave their children presents and opportunities. Half of Jonathan's library was made of books from Neville Lipton. Jonathan had gone on trips to museums and galleries sponsored by Neville Lipton. Jonathan placed a mark of authenticity on anything by saying, 'Mr Lipton says.'

'He has no business living in this neighbourhood,' Amara had told Chinechelum. 'I think he's doing it to make a political statement.'

'If he is, then that's extremely paternalistic,' Chinechelum had said. Or had she? She wasn't sure now what her response had been. She did recall being both vaguely fascinated and repulsed by how much Neville Lipton seemed to know about Nigeria, rattling off the history with dates during their brief conversation. And so when she ran into him on the street, on her way to explore London once again, he remembered her and kissed both her cheeks and noticed that she had cut her hair since the last time he saw her.

'Let's have lunch together, shall we? Come with me,' he said, already moving and expecting her to follow. Chinechelum did. This was what living life again was about, after all, giving in to impulse, embracing spontaneity. Going off to lunch with Amara's elderly neighbour whom she hardly knew. This was *life*.

'I'll take you to the Traveller's Club. That's a lovely jacket you have on, so we won't have any difficulty being let in. They have a quite annoying dress code, you see.'

'Really,' Chinechelum said, surprised that he thought her old jacket was lovely, and later as they were led into the ornate interior of the Traveller's Club, she looked around at the men seated at the tables to see what they were wearing. She had expected to see bow ties. But she saw mostly suits that seemed staid next to Neville Lipton's well-tailored jacket lined in bright orange-and-green kente print. It was clear that Neville Lipton was different from the men here and that he embraced his being different. She imagined him, in another life, going off to explore Africa and returning with triumphant skins, with stories of surprisingly articulate natives.

'It's so stuffy in here,' she said after they had been seated. She meant it figuratively and he understood and laughed.

'You have such a lovely voice,' he said, leaning closer. 'If only you didn't have that American inflection to your speech.' He was staring at her. His eyes were so blue they looked painted-on and his hair was a startling white, receding from a finely wrinkled face. As they waited for their orders, he gave her a brief history of the Traveller's Club, a monologue on the necessity of the monarchy, a scathing attack on the misguided asses who wanted to outlaw fox hunting. He called her 'dear one' and 'darling girl' and used the adverb 'iniquitously'. He made her laugh when he said 'fuck' with the old-world Englishness of an Oxbridge octogenarian. He seemed determined to introduce her to everyone that passed, even the waiters, and after he had said her name in a quick, indistinguishable mumble, he added, always, 'She's Nigerian.'

Right after their orders came, a man with hair sticking out of his nose came up to them, glanced at Chinechelum and asked Neville, 'Who's the dusky beauty with you?'

Neville introduced her, told the man that she was Nigerian and added that she was a poet and an assistant professor in America.

'How do you do?' the man asked her.

Chinechelum said nothing. The man was smiling.

'It's a pleasure meeting you,' the man said, raising his voice slightly, as if he imagined she might not have heard him the first time. Still, Chinechelum said nothing. The silence stretched out. She felt the tension, revelled in the awkwardness. This was the old Chinechelum and she was comfortable with it. The man muttered something to Neville and then moved on.

'Dear girl!' Neville said, in a theatrical whisper. 'Whatever did you do that for?'

'*Dusky beauty.*'

'Well. He was complimenting you.'

'No, he was complimenting *you*. Like one would compliment somebody who had a good racehorse.'

'The old chap meant no harm, in fact he would give anything to be sitting in my place.' Neville chuckled and Chinechelum felt the urge to throw her glass of water in his face. She ran a finger over the rim of her glass instead and said, pleasantly, 'You know, Mr Lipton, I think all of you here are tight-assed old men.'

Neville stared at her for a moment before he burst out laughing. 'Goodness, Chichilum…'

'What did you call me?'

He looked at her as if he was not sure what she had said.
'My name is Chinechelum, Mr Lipton. *Chi-ne-che-lum.*'
He repeated her name a few times, with the earnest expression
of one eager to get it right although he mauled it each time. Then
he asked, 'What does it mean, by the way?'
'God Thinks For Me.'
'Does it? I have a friend from Zimbabwe, a Shona, whose name
means The Fire of God. Interesting. I did wonder if God possessing
fire was desirable or not.' He sipped his water. 'God Thinks For Me.
It doesn't suit you much, does it?'
'Why?'
'Why? Darling one, it does suggests passivity, doesn't it, and there
is nothing passive about you. My goodness, you don't have one
deferential bone in your body.'
He sounded surprised. She examined the coffee-coloured age spots
on his face for a while. And then she said, 'You sound as if I should.'
Was it her imagination or did he blush, this hard-boiled worldly
old man? 'You're terribly touchy, aren't you, on the subject of race?
Africans aren't, unless of course they've lived in America.'
'You seem to know everything about Africans.'
He reached out and took her hand. 'Don't be like that, darling one.'
And she didn't know why, but she started talking about Ikeadi.
Perhaps it was to tell Neville Lipton that he had no right to tell her
how to be, about race, or about anything else. Perhaps there was
no reason to it, only that the words came out of her, chased one
another past her lips.
First, before she told him about the night Ikeadi was shot, she told
him what Ikeadi used to say. That he and she were destined. That if
somebody drained the streams of both their ancestral villages, their
names would be written on the riverbed, intertwined. After he was
shot, she had wanted to go back to Nigeria, to his hometown of
Umunnachi and her hometown of Abba, and she wanted to jump into
the streams at both places and drain them somehow and see what was
written there, see if Ikeadi's name would now appear in crippled letters.
She told Neville Lipton about Ikeadi's temper, that he broke beer
bottles when he was angry; about Ikeadi's idealism, that he joined
causes and marched and picketed, that his father owned an often-
empty home in West Hartford but he chose to live in a minuscule

The Grief of Strangers

apartment in East Hartford, which he paid for himself, and that he was in front of that apartment building, about to unlock his door when the police cars arrived. Three men. Three white men. Later, during the trial, they said they thought he was pulling a gun. And she sat in the courtroom and cried because the vestibule in front of his apartment door was so narrow and it was inconceivable how he had evaded so many of those forty bullets. And even later she had wished that Ikeadi was the Haitian man who was all over the news for a while, the one who had only been sodomized with a dirty broom handle by a policeman. At least that man, the Haitian, had been left whole.

Finally, she told Neville Lipton, 'When Ikeadi lost the use of his body, it was the end of fall, and two days later it was snowing and weeks later spring came and it rained and the seasons kept changing, as if nothing had happened to Ikeadi. I kept waiting for something to happen. You know? I just kept waiting.'

She put her fork down, angry that she had talked to this undeserving man about Ikeadi, angry that Ikeadi was there right now in the nursing home in Hartford, paralysed, and now so clinically depressed he could no longer blink when she arrived. Or he chose to no longer blink.

But she was also exhilarated that she had finally talked about Ikeadi, that she could talk to an acquaintance she wasn't even sure she liked about the man for whom she had kept her life on hold for nine years.

Odin had spoken so highly of the restaurant he took her to the next day that Chinechelum was determined to like it no matter what. It was very modern-chic, with chrome decor and wide gleaming spaces and a menu carved on to thin metal sheets.

'This decor is art, isn't it? But it's a different art from yours, from your poetry,' Odin said.

'I suppose so,' she murmured. There was something different about Odin today, or was it—whatever it was—there the last time she saw him only that she hadn't looked closely enough to notice? She didn't want to talk about her art, the expression 'your art' was troubling enough, and so she said, 'Odin doesn't sound like an Igbo name.'

'It's Odinchezo, but I made it shorter, you know, it's easier for these people.'

Chimamanda Ngozi Adichie

'Oh,' Chinechelum said and looked down at her food, strips of grilled fish so painstakingly arranged she felt bad having to disrupt the pattern by eating them. She remembered how she and Ikeadi used to criticize her Aunty Ngolika for calling her son 'Bob' although his name was Nnaemeka, and then saying it was because of 'these people'. 'What people?' she wanted to ask Odin. You didn't have to deny your heritage and then blame some phantom people for a choice that you had made.

'How's the fish?' Odin asked. He looked nervous, that was it. Nervous.

'It tastes as interesting as it looks,' she said.

Odin placed his fork down. 'There is something I haven't told you. Something you should know.'

'Yes?'

Odin cleared his throat loudly. 'I have a son. He's six. His mother has custody but I see him every other week.'

There was a short stretch of silence between them; even the people at other tables seemed to stop speaking. 'I didn't want to tell you earlier,' Odin said. 'I didn't want to tell you anything that would make you back off too early.' He was avoiding her eyes: looking above her head and then swiftly back to focus on his food. She thought he suddenly looked so much younger, so much more vulnerable. And she wanted to tell him that it was okay, that we all are allowed, should be allowed, to put down our load, to untie the baggage we carry, only when we want to. Only when we are ready to.

'It's all right,' she said.

'I just knew you were different.' Odin leaned closer towards her, across the table. 'I think lately I've been wondering where my life has gone. I think you being in my life can help me find a balance.'

She held her fork in wonder. How could he possibly know that? How could he possibly know that it was *her*, just *her*, who would make him happy?

She felt the urge to tell him about Ikeadi, to let him know that she, too, had something she hadn't told him. But she didn't. She didn't have to. It was freeing to realize that he didn't have to know, and even more freeing to realize, sitting there and looking at his clean jaw and his deep-brown eyes, that it would never work between them, that he would eventually be connected to another Nigerian woman unburdened by a new desire for life. A woman who, unlike her, would not long for *spontaneity*, for *realness*, for a connection that was unchoreographed, such as meeting strangers in a Starbucks cafe.

B ack in Connecticut, she took a taxi from the airport, huddled in the back because the heater was taking too long. The air was still; the sides of the road were covered with piles of snow and the piercing whiteness hurt her eyes. On the news, she heard that some children had been killed in Massachusetts, that they were playing on a frozen lake when the surface broke and they sank in. They drowned in sub-zero water: three little boys aged between seven and nine.

Chinechelum closed her eyes, but she didn't cry. ☐

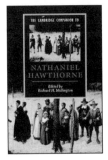

GRANTA

THE VIEW FROM THIS END

Alexandra Fuller in Livingston, Zambia, October 1993

The View from this End

My first rainy season in Zambia, in 1993, was one of the wettest in decades. By December, the city had flooded and cars drove down Cha Cha Cha Road, right past the government buildings in the centre of Lusaka, up to their hubs and higher in brown sewage-rich water. The privies and drains and the streets and slums, long piled high and overspilling with human waste and refuse, sent their excess belching into the streets. We walked with our skirts held up around our hips, our shoes dangling from the ends of our fingers, and our lips pressed tight against the flies and stench.

The new cholera lorries rocked past us with dangerous urgency, spraying pedestrians and cars with mud and leaving behind them the faint, lingering scent of antiseptic and the nostril-widening scent of ancient disease.

Cholera. Goes with disease words like plague, pox, chigger, delirium.

Those unmistakable white lorries with blue logos painted on their doors and flashing yellow lights on their roofs—there must have been a dozen in the city at that time—had been donated by foreign aid groups. They were shiny under the thin, splattered glaze of mud; polite with a generous aura of Europe. But the bodies in the backs of the lorries were all Zambian. Women and men, crouched over each other, wretched with infection, holding their leaking bodies in check with bright bolts of cloth across their mouths, over their heads. They were people in mourning for themselves.

Every evening the lorries trundled out to Leopard's Hill Road, where the big cemetery lay, bringing with them the dead and the high-wailing relatives of the dead; the ululating women; the sombre men beneath crush-rimmed hats; the wide-eyed children. The cemetery was already spilling beyond capacity with the wasted bodies of Aids victims. Now it was overwhelmed by the carcasses spawned by cholera. In places, big pits had been dug, lime-sprinkled. We were like a people covering up a war crime.

I asked the groom, Day-Freddy, 'Where do they take the sick people?'

He said, 'To the cholera clinics.'

'You mean the hospitals?'

Day-Freddy frowned, 'I don't know.' He shrugged again. 'You should know.'

'Why should I know?'

Alexandra Fuller

'You are the one to write for the paper.'

I stared at Day-Freddy. We were sitting outside on the back veranda after our morning ride, drinking tea. 'Well, I do write for the paper.' But not about potentially troublesome issues like cholera. Not since I got into trouble with the article about the Minister of the Environment. I had interviewed him for a new, independent paper. He was famously corrupt, obviously inept and without curiosity or intelligence. The day the article was published, my husband Charlie was pulled into a government official's office and told to keep me under control.

Charlie had shrugged, 'Me keep her under control?'

The official had swung back on his chair and said, casually, 'Your work permit can be revoked at any time, Mr Ross.'

So now I wrote about the great success of Zambia's tobacco crops in the north and the country's potential for tourism in the east and a series of canoe trips I had taken on the middle section of the Zambezi River. I wrote gently about Zambia's rich wildlife, its heritage of forests.

'Anyway, we Zambians die like chickens,' said Day-Freddy, soaking a thick doorstop of bread in his sweet, milky tea. 'Maybe it's not news for the paper.' He took a mouthful of soggy bread and told me, 'More people die of cholera. So? What's the news in that?' He swallowed and added, 'And you can't write this story.'

'Why not?'

Day-Freddy drained his tea and turned his cup over, flicking tea leaves and drops on the ground. 'Because you have fear,' he said.

The next morning Day-Freddy and I drove into the second-class district to buy maize bran for the horses. We were on our way home when a cholera lorry, swaying dangerously as it avoided potholes, tore past us. On impulse, I turned across the road and banked off the steep edge where tarmac had receded to expose red gums of eroded soil.

'What are you doing, Madam?' asked Day-Freddy, clutching the edge of the seat.

'We're going to follow the cholera lorry,' I told him. 'We're going to find a cholera clinic.'

The lorry led us out of Lusaka, past Soweto market with its stalls of stolen car parts and second-hand clothes, and deep into the centre of George Compound. Day-Freddy kept shaking his head, 'Very dangerous,' he told me. 'This is not a good plan, Madam.'

'Why not?'

'You are white, you are a woman. They will attack you. They will steal this pickup,' his eyes rolled wildly, 'they will beat me.'

'Don't be silly.'

'Look around here. They are poor, you are rich. You are crazy.'

'You're afraid,' I told him.

Day-Freddy nodded.

We were spinning through thick mud. House spilled upon house, each one made of more imaginative and desperate material than the last; houses of cloth sacks, plastic bags, road signs, cardboard and unravelled tyres. Tin roofs, or roofs made up of patched-together stop signs were held down with rocks. Great piles of refuse as high as the car towered next to each house on either side of the road. At times the water was so deep it threatened to seep under the doors and on to our feet. Day-Freddy pressed his shoes firmly against the dashboard and wrinkled his nose. 'How can people live like dogs?'

'It's not their fault.'

'I didn't say it was a fault, Madam. I was simply asking this: How can people live like this?'

'I don't know.'

'I'm not getting out to push,' Day-Freddy informed me, 'if you get stuck.'

I kept the revs high, clutched the steering wheel tightly and followed closely in the wake left by the cholera lorry, hoping I would not accidentally slide off the road altogether. Children balanced high and victorious on top of the piles of refuse called after me, '*Mzungu! Mzungu!*' and waggled their hips at me.

We stopped, finally, at a school that had undergone a hasty conversion into a cholera clinic. Day-Freddy wouldn't leave the car. 'I've read the posters,' he told me. 'You will catch cholera and die if you step in there.' He covered his nose and mouth with his hands and made a face. 'I think you can catch it through breathing.' His voice was muffled and anxious.

'No you won't,' I scolded him. 'Only if you don't wash your hands.' But the smell was overpowering when I opened the car door and for a moment I hesitated. Then I saw Day-Freddy's expression and I stepped gingerly out of the car.

'Can I help you?' asked a man who was stirring a huge drum of yellow liquid at the foot of the steps.

'I was just...' I cleared my throat, 'I was wondering if you'd let me look around?'

'Around?'

'Yes. I've seen the cholera lorries, I was just—'

'Who are you?'

'No one.'

The man frowned at me suspiciously.

'I was just curious, that's all.'

Behind me, still in the pickup, I heard Day-Freddy snort with derision. I turned around to glare at him. He quickly covered his face again.

'I was thinking... I write for the paper.'

The man stopped stirring the liquid in the drum and frowned at me again, fiercely this time. 'Which paper? No journalists allowed,' he said. He put down the broom handle with which he was stirring the liquid in the drum and made shooing motions at me. 'You must go.'

'But don't you think people should know what is happening here?'

'What people?'

'I mean people who read the papers.'

'The people who read the papers already know what is going on,' the man said, returning to his drum.

I squinted back against the sun at Day-Freddy who was flapping frantically at the air, trying to get flies out of the cab.

'What's in the drum?' I asked the man.

'Clothes,' the man replied, 'contaminated clothes. We are supposed to burn them, but how can you burn clothes if they are all somebody has to wear?'

There were over a hundred people in that school turned cholera clinic, most of them naked but for a single covering of cloth. There were not enough cholera beds (stretchers with holes cut into them, with buckets under the holes), or beds of any description, so patients shared stretchers. Their bottoms could not fit over the holes, with two of them like that, and they were shitting on one another. Other patients had been lined up on soggy cardboard on the veranda where intravenous drips hanging from washing lines fed into upturned arms. Babies slept in the nook of their sick mothers' arms. Vomit and shit, like watery rice, were mopped up from the floor, scraped off the beds, sloshed off the cardboard sheets, by a nurse wearing a plastic apron and gumboots.

There was a single flush toilet which had long since ceased to flush—its contents slopped out on to the veranda. The two long-drops in the yard wafted disease and exhaustion, flooded and sagging precariously. The morgue was a black tent, steaming in the afternoon sun, next to the long-drops. It was from the morgue that the pervasive, sweet-rotten smell was coming.

This was not a humanitarian disaster on the vast scale Africa is so capable of producing, just a heartless indignity imposed upon a few thousand unlucky Zambians, one hundred of whom happened to be dribbling slowly to death right here.

While I was there, the cholera lorry left with bodies from the morgue and another appeared with freshly ill victims.

While I was there, a patient was brought from a distant village in a wheelbarrow by his relatives and had to be helped on to a corner of cardboard, where he died before the orderly could put the needle of the intravenous drip into his arm.

A baby, kept with its sick mother on a cholera bed in one of the old classrooms, died of pneumonia. It lay like a sodden comma, curled up against its mother, and no one realized it was dead until she began to bleat, her trilling thin with dehydration and despair. A pretty young nurse, in a white uniform with black gumboots and a white plastic apron, held the tiny body away from her as she hurried to the morgue.

I was only there an hour.

I drove home too fast, grim and guilty with what I had seen. Day-Freddy occupied himself trying to hunt down and kill flies.

'They'll bring the illness back to us,' he said, his voice squeaky with hysteria.

'Oh, don't be silly.'

'If a fly lands on you, you'll be sick. Sure, sure.'

When we got back to Lilayi Road, I left the pickup running and ran inside to collect blankets, clothes, towels, soap, aspirin, tins of food and shoes. I put them into cardboard boxes which I carried out to the vehicle.

'What are you doing?' asked Day-Freddy.

'You saw those people.' I could still smell the clinic in my hair, on my skin. I had been made to wash my hands and feet in a drum of caustic antiseptic before I could leave the clinic. The tyres of my car had been doused with the same yellow fluid.

'But I need these things,' Day-Freddy said plaintively, fingering a pile of towels.

'No you don't.'

'All of this?' he asked, holding up some tennis shoes.

'Yes,' I said firmly. 'You've had enough from me, wouldn't you say.'

Day-Freddy returned my accusing look steadily. 'You're too soft-soft,' he told me.

'That may be. Or maybe I'm not soft-soft enough.'

'They'll just sell everything,' he said, sulkily.

'So? Don't you?'

Day-Freddy sulked.

Two weeks later I could still smell the clinic when the wind lifted my hair. And my cholera article was rejected by the independent newspaper whose editor had recently been arrested and accused of slander towards a government minister.

Day-Freddy and I rode the horses up to the game farm at the top of the road and turned east into the rising sun. We were smiling into the cool breeze picked up off the previous night's rain.

'Race you,' I told him, which was no competition. He was on the faster mare, and he was a gutsier rider. 'Give me a head start and watch for antbear holes.' I trotted ahead. Gozzy tossed his head and flecked my leg with saliva. I could hear Day-Freddy muttering softly, reassuring Kalamo. 'On your marks,' I shouted over my shoulder, gathering up the reins and crouching forward. 'Get set,' I let Gozzy's rear end bunch up under the saddle. 'Go!'

Kalamo streaked past us before we had reached the first gate; by then I had lost all but the most rudimentary control of Gozzy. I was holding on hard, muscles tight with crouching, my breathing loud and rasping in my ears. I pulled up next to Day-Freddy, who was grinning like a fool, panting, his face shining with sweat even in the cool morning. 'I won, Madam.'

'You won.' I leaned forward on my saddle and looked up at him, panting. I was wondering if I'd eaten something a bit off the night before. Suddenly I didn't feel very well. Day-Freddy swam in front of me. His smile melting into his face—dripping red, black, white like smudging paint.

'Jesus, Freddy.' I was still breathing hard. 'I think I'm...I think I need to...' I slid off Gozzy and my legs buckled.

'Madam?'

Day-Freddy jumped off the mare and the two horses sauntered off to graze. Day-Freddy crouched next to me, tried to hold me up. I retched and yellow vomit splattered out on to the green Rhodes grass and dribbled down my chin.

'Oh,' cried Day-Freddy, dropping my shoulders and letting me fall over, 'you have the cholera, Madam! You have for sure the cholera.' He held his hands up in the air in horror and stepped back from me.

I shook my head, but could not speak. My body was racked with another bout of retching. When I could catch my breath I said, 'Fetch the horses now, let's ride home.'

'But you are sick, Madam.'

'It's okay, Freddy, don't call the cholera lorry yet.' But I was only half joking.

The rainy season leaked on through March, by which time I had forgotten what it felt like to live without nausea and exhaustion. For hours at a time, I watched rain cry down the windows in the bedroom. Heat and humidity settled like breath somewhere north of my stomach. I began to have fantasies about strawberries and snow and chocolate breakfast cereal, none of which were available but which all seemed to promise a reprieve from my condition.

At weekday lunchtimes, the *mzungu* doctor in Lusaka was usually to be found drinking deeply of South African wine at the Marco Polo restaurant, indifferent to the constraints of the conventional lunch hour. He didn't bother to remove his white clinical coat or his stethoscope when leaving his offices at noon. This being Zambia, a medical emergency could arise at any moment. Surgery using knife and fork and red wine.

He was the acknowledged authority on malaria, bilharzia and rabies, and though he couldn't treat you, he would tell you—without frills—if you were among the one-in-three Zambians to have acquired HIV.

He carelessly dispensed the few medications available to him for the treatment of dysentery, tuberculosis, ringworm, giardia, syphilis, witchcraft and tick fever. But he did not consider the possibility of pregnancy a medical condition.

For the third time in three months, the pregnancy test administered by the doctor's nurse had come back without a red stripe in the right-hand window. 'Are you sure the tests aren't out of date? Perhaps they've expired.' I cleared my throat and the doctor looked at his watch again. I was making him late for his customary bottle of South African wine. I thought about how else I might phrase this and at last I said, 'You may want to just have a quick peek up there. Just to make sure.'

'A peek?' said the doctor with distaste.

'A little peek,' I tried.

Which he wouldn't do. Especially before lunch.

'You have an IUD installed, no?'

'Well, yes.'

'So?'

So, for the third time in as many months he declared my pregnancy hysterical and for the third time in as many months I waved my gratitude and farewell at him, mouth covered, and hurried off to the clinic loos where I vomited noisily and prolifically, to the distress of the patients waiting for their prescriptions at the pharmacy.

'I must have a tummy bug after all,' I told Charlie.

But then the hard lump of baby in my belly became impossible to deny. And I must have been throwing up for a reason.

If it wasn't cholera. Which it wasn't. And if I hadn't had my period for three months, which I hadn't.

Dad, up from the farm, said, 'Well of course, you're in calf.'

'But the pregnancy tests came back negative.'

'Tests? Pah.'

'Damn.'

Dad lit a cigarette. 'Don't worry. Half of all heifers lose their first take.'

'No, it's not that,' I said. 'No, Dad. I want the baby.'

'Oh.' He was embarrassed and didn't know what to say. He stirred more sugar into his tea. 'Well, then...' Dad was trying, in his rough way, to protect me from what he thought I didn't know. 'Ja, well don't be disappointed, that's all. You know, if... It's common to have a practice run.'

I didn't have the heart to tell him that I had already had a practice run.

Years ago I took care of that. On an anonymous, thin, plastic-sheeted bed, a stranger's white-gloved hands in a Canadian hospital took care of that. I didn't tell Dad that I cried for days into a friend's pillow and smoked all my friend's cigarettes and bled into his toilet until he came and carried me, inexpertly, to bed, and let me bleed on to his sheets. He was not the father of the child I had chosen to lose, just an old friend with a car and a basement apartment near campus and a big heart.

The old friend, holding me, had said, 'I had a hamster I really loved when I was a kid. And one day I hugged the little fucker to death, by mistake.' He stroked my head. 'So I know how you feel.' Then we put a towel under me and he said, 'Shit, how much blood is there to lose? You need fluids,' and fetched me a cold beer.

I told Dad that there were worse things than finding out you're pregnant.

We decided I should drive through the border at Chirundu and up to Harare, Zimbabwe for the advice of a medical expert. We had to stop periodically so I could throw up: after the winding Zambezi escarpment and at the urine-smelling border post and behind the diesel-belching buses at Cloud's End.

The Zimbabwean gynaecologist confirmed via ultrasound that I was pregnant. He showed me where the baby lay, a little pulse in my womb. I looked up at the pictures on the doctor's wall describing foetal development and I imagined my baby, her tiny fists curled in a Black Power salute ('Free Nelson Mandela! Send him home to So-wet-oh!') and then the doctor showed me where the intrauterine device might hinder her growth.

Alexandra Fuller

'If you leave the IUD in situ, you risk losing the baby. Or worse.'
'What can be worse?'
The doctor shrugged, an African educated in London, with the schooling of the West, but his own people's matter-of-factness about life, death, loss. 'It's for you to decide. Perhaps some…impediment to growth.'
'And if I have IUD removed?'
'You still risk losing the baby.'
I stared up at the wall, at the little defiant fist on the smudgy black-and-white photograph of someone else's baby. I said, 'I don't think I'll lose this one.'
Then I offered my arm to the clinic's nurse and blood was siphoned off to test for HIV, syphilis, gonorrhoea.
Charlie had gone outside to the car and I went out to look for him. There were other potential fathers kicking their heels in the dust and smoking cigarettes, leaned up against farm pickups while their pregnant wives were inside the whitewashed walls of the clinic.
'Well, I'm definitely pregnant.' I crossed my arms and looked away so Charlie couldn't see my tears and I said, 'Bugger, bugger, bugger. He says I might lose it.'
Charlie reached out for me again and this time I let him rock me against his shoulder. And then morning sickness took over and I fought my way out of his embrace to throw up in the gynaecologist's beautiful orange cannas.

We chose a small clinic in a village east of Harare to have the IUD removed. I didn't want to lose the baby, but if I did, I wanted to bury her somewhere I would find her again. Somewhere small and quiet and where I could come back and find the flowers I'd planted for her.
I was bedded next to an old-timer in a tiny ward for two that overlooked a pine forest and a comforting, bright new garden of English country flowers: nasturtiums, rhododendrons, lavender and roses.
'What you here for?' asked my neighbour, patting her covers happily and eyeing me over the top of her glasses.
'I'm pregnant,' I said.
'Well, you don't look it,' she said suspiciously.
'That's because I'm not very far along.'

'Good, then we won't have any squawking kids in here any time soon.'

'No.'

The old lady had been prescribed sherry before lunch, 'To stimulate my appetite,' she explained. ' I can tell you something else, I haven't had so much fun...' She sipped her sherry appreciatively. 'Underestimated for the digestion,' she confided. Then added, 'I can't stand babies.' She offered me a sip from her glass which I declined weakly, nauseated. 'They won't let me smoke though.'

'Oh.'

'Call me old-fashioned, but I don't have a problem with smoking. Do you? You wouldn't mind if I smoked, would you?'

I grunted.

The pre-op drugs were starting to take effect. My mouth was dry and my legs felt as if they were floating.

'I hate visiting day,' said my neighbour with sudden vehemence. 'They all come to see me and sit on my bed and I can't read. I can't knit. And they're so boring.'

'Who?' I asked feebly.

'My children. Their children. The whole bloody lot of them. They whinge.'

The last thing I heard and saw before they wheeled me into the operating room was the old lady, raising her sherry glass in salute and asking loudly, urgently, 'From what? You didn't say from what? What are you pregnant from?' and looking around the place as if expecting an attack from an unknown quarter.

Charlie was there when I woke up. For a man not given to emotion, he looked close to tears as he said, 'It's going to be okay.'

'I'm still pregnant?'

'So far. They're going to give you something to help you sleep. I'll come get you tomorrow.'

I drifted in and out for the next twelve hours, unable to struggle out of the deep, drugged sleep completely, even as I fought it. During the night, a long, green snake found its way into our ward. My old neighbour, assisted by a man whom I vaguely remember as being attached by a pole to an intravenous drip, killed it with a walking stick and draped it on the end of a broom handle.

It had only been a poor, fat house snake.
The doctor told me to take it easy for the next few days.
'Any idea when she's due?' I asked.
'How do you know it's a she?'
I shrugged. 'Just do,' I replied.
The doctor sighed and pressed her hands to my belly. 'You're three months along, I'd say.' She shut her eyes and felt along the ridges of my ribs. 'The end of August,' she announced, 'maybe early September.'

We came back in late August to wait for the baby. We stayed in the highlands for a fortnight, hiking in the relief of cool, pine-scented air and then the doctor decided that there was no more room for the baby to be in my great swinging belly, it was time for us to persuade her to come out.

The local vicar's wife was found to have the same blood group as mine and was told to stand by for a couple of days, veins at the ready, in case I should need her blood. A seventy-year-old, tennis-playing farmer's wife who had, forty years earlier, delivered twins (vaginally and without medical intervention or pain relief) was summoned to give me a few pointers on the birthing process. She kept her lesson brief, swinging her tennis racquet around experimentally all the time. 'Piece of old tackie, really,' she said, sending an imaginary lob over my shoulder. 'Women have been doing this since Adam and Eve, so just remember—you're not doing anything special.' *Slam!* 'Just keep breathing, don't bother with the hollering, and you'll be fine.'

'Thank you.'

She turned to Charlie, 'I've rafted the Zambezi,' she announced, twisting to execute an air-backhand. 'That's what childbirth is like,' she informed me unhelpfully, 'wave after wave.' *Wa-boom!* 'And then you hit an eddy.'

'I see.'

'An enema will really help get this labour going,' the Shona midwife told me. I was already pinned to the bed with pain and, as far as I had been told, we were not even close to a cigar. The midwife loomed in and out of my range of vision, which was mostly the pale blue tent made by the blanket hung between my knees and a high barred window that leaked in a pale, spring light.

'A what?'

SAVE UP TO £50!

Each quarterly issue of *Granta* features a rich variety of stories, in fiction, memoir, reportage and photography—often collected under a theme, like those shown overleaf. Each issue is produced as a high-quality paperback book, because writing this good deserves nothing less. Subscribers get *Granta* delivered to them at home, at a substantial discount. Why not join them? Or give a subscription to a friend, relative or colleague. (Or, given these low prices, do both!)

GRANTA 'ESSENTIAL READING'

OBSERVER

ORDER FORM

I'D LIKE TO SUBSCRIBE FOR MYSELF FOR: ⃝ 1 year (4 issues) at just £26.95   **£13 saving**
⃝ 2 years (8 issues) at just £50   **£30 saving**
⃝ 3 years (12 issues) at just £70   **£50 saving**
START THE SUBSCRIPTION WITH ⃝ this issue ⃝ next issue

I'D LIKE TO GIVE A SUBSCRIPTION FOR: ⃝ 1 year (4 issues) at just £26.95
⃝ 2 years (8 issues) at just £50
⃝ 3 years (12 issues) at just £70
START THE SUBSCRIPTION WITH ⃝ this issue ⃝ next issue

MY DETAILS (please supply even if ordering a gift): Mr/Ms/Mrs/Miss

Country   Postcode

GIFT RECIPIENT'S DETAILS (if applicable): Mr/Ms/Mrs/Miss

Country   Postcode

04LBG88

TOTAL* £ _____ paid by ⃝ £ cheque enclosed (to 'Granta') ⃝ Visa/Mastercard/AmEx:

card no: __ __ __ __ __ __ __ __ __ __ __ __ __ __ __ __

expires: __ __ / __ __ signature:

* POSTAGE. The prices stated include UK postage. For the rest of Europe, please add £8 (per year). For the rest of the world, please add £15 (per year). DATA PROTECTION. Please tick here if you do not want to receive occasional mailings from compatible publishers. ⃝

➟ **POST** ('Freepost' in the UK) to: Granta, 'Freepost', 2/3 Hanover Yard, Noel Road, London N1 8BR. **PHONE/FAX:** In the UK: FreeCall 0500 004 033 (phone & fax); outside the UK: tel 44 (0)20 7704 9776, fax 44 (0)20 7704 0474 **EMAIL:** subs@granta.com

'Come on,' she said, producing a length of thin red hosepipe, 'roll over on your side.'

'Oh my God, no, you're not going to…'

Mum, who had driven down with us from Zambia to help me deliver the baby, grinned unhelpfully.

'Mu-um!'

She said, 'I heard of a movie star that got a gerbil stuck in his bottom once. Just think about that. That's got to be worse than an enema.'

'Out,' I said, glaring at Mum and Charlie, 'both of you out!' I groaned through a contraction.

'Keep an eye out for gerbils, ha, ha.'

'Not funny, Mum.'

The door slammed behind my mother and husband.

'And stay there,' I shouted, 'till I tell you.'

The midwife said, 'This is a good remedy for a slow labour.'

'It's humiliating is what it is.' I had imagined a placid labour, set to gentle music while I smiled bravely through the pain and effortlessly produced a perfect baby.

She laughed, 'Humiliating? My dear, a day from now you will know what true humiliation is.'

'Oh God.' I held on to the edge of the bed and gritted my teeth.

By four o'clock in the afternoon the baby had been stuck for hours. The doctor put the kettle on. 'Keep pushing,' she told me, 'and you'll get this baby out in time for tea.' Now that anything I had to say had been reduced to words of one syllable, Mum and Charlie had been called back into the room. I grabbed Mum's arm on one side and the midwife's arm on the other, dug my chin into my chest and pushed. Charlie peered hopefully at my bottom.

'Nope,' he announced.

I came up for air. 'Fuck off. Please.'

Charlie got out of range.

Now the kettle was boiling. The doctor scooped tea leaves into a pot and poured hot water over them, the steamy, sweet smell of brewing tea adding to the close, sweaty atmosphere in the room.

I dug my nails into Mum's hand. 'I don't think I can do this,' but then another contraction came and I pushed into the endless, deep pain of it.

The doctor glanced at the teapot ruefully. 'Time to get this baby out,' she told me, rolling up her sleeves. She brought out a knife and something that looked like a toilet plunger. I shut my eyes.

'Just keep breathing,' said Charlie, re-emerging from his corner. 'Fuck off.'

Mum held on to my shoulders and the midwife held on to my legs (like a cow, I thought), and the doctor pulled. If she'd brought out a rope and chain and pulled the child out with the help of a tractor, I would not have been surprised.

I thought of the men at the dip pulling a difficult calf from a cow, singing as they heaved, '*Potsi, piri, tatu, ini.*'

Somewhere far away, somewhere else in the hospital, I heard a woman scream.

Mum said, 'Shhhhh.' And I realized the scream had come from me.

'Push,' said the Shona midwife.

I pushed, the doctor pulled and Mum held on.

Then the baby was on my stomach and I was crying. She was long-limbed, dark-haired, blood-smeared and perfect. She had lips like rosebuds. I put my arms over her and I knew, suddenly and unexpectedly, that I had been put on this earth for one reason only: to give life to this child.

'Cup of tea?' asked the midwife, propping a cup next to me on the bed.

'That'll do you good,' said Mum, 'put a bit of sugar in it.'

'I hate sugar in my tea.'

At a basin in the corner of the ward, a fourteen-year-old girl who had come into the clinic hours after me was preparing to leave. She was up, fully dressed, and was bathing and dressing her new baby. If she can do it, I can do it, I thought. I felt for the edge of my bed and swung my feet on to the floor. Supporting myself against the bed frame, I had a brief vision of the young girl's face and her pink-clothed baby. Then a swimming and indistinct sense that the floor was slipping away from me and rolling up to become the ceiling. Blackness rushed into my head and I was on the floor.

Mum fetched a basin of water and a bar of soap. 'I'll give you a bed bath,' she said, 'you can try getting up tomorrow.' The nurse came through to see how I was getting on and gave me a little white pill to help with the pain. As I drifted out of my mind in a comfortably drugged state I asked, slurring a little, 'What's the pill?'

'Valium,' said the nurse, drawing the curtains, 'we find most…ladies need a little something to calm them after birth.'

I sighed and sank back against the pillows. 'The baby?' I asked, indistinctly.

'She's fine,' someone murmured.

I heard Mum say to Charlie, 'Ready for something a bit stiffer than tea?'

Charlie leaned over me and planted a kiss on my forehead. A cigar leered out of his top pocket. 'Well done, babe.'

It wasn't until much later, in the middle of the night, that I struggled out of my fog and lay breathing into the darkness trying to remember where I was. Why did I feel as if I'd been torn in half. Jesus Christ! The baby! Where did I put the baby! I patted the bed next to me and groped wildly around the bedclothes. 'Nurse!' No one came. I swung out of bed and hurried (clutching my bottom which felt as if it might slip out on to the floor) towards a mild light at the end of a dark passage.

'Is the baby here?'

The nurse on duty smelled of cigarettes and coffee. She was knitting, her feet comfortably propped up on the desk in front of her. 'What are you doing out of bed, sweetie?'

'I'm looking for my baby.'

'You can't have her until morning.'

'It is morning,' I said, letting myself behind the desk and looking around, fighting the panic that had swelled in my chest. 'Where did you put her?'

'It's okay, darling. You go back and sleep. It's the last bit of shut-eye you'll be getting for a while.'

'Where is she?' I insisted, planting myself firmly in front of the nurse and holding myself together. I'd seen a cow with a prolapsed uterus on the farm once.

The nurse counted her stitches and put her knitting down reluctantly. 'Come.'

The baby was alone in a plastic box, with a bright light bulb hanging over her. 'The light keeps her warm,' said the nurse. Like baby chickens.

Alexandra Fuller

I scooped up the swaddled infant from the plastic box.
'I promise we can keep her here for you. I've been feeding her
sugared water.' The nurse sounded defensive, a little offended.
'It's all right,' I said. 'I'll take her now.'
I held the soft sleeping thing up to my face and inhaled the fresh
breath of her new lungs, the soft-kitten-blood smell of her recent
birth.
I went back to bed, undressed myself and unrolled the baby, holding
her next to my skin. She nestled into my breast, her rosebud mouth
opened and closed over my nipple. I shut my eyes and closed my arms
around her. 'I promise I won't let you go,' I told the baby. We fell asleep
like that, both of us naked, with her mouth soft and wet over my
nipple and her breathing warm and steady against my neck.

In October, at the end of the six-month dry season, the spray from
Victoria Falls that thundered for a mile into the sky in the wetter
months barely puffed up to the lip of the gorge. We had moved to
Livingstone, close to the Zambezi River. The sky was low and rolling
with bruised, unproductive storm clouds and the air was grey-yellow
with wildfires and dust. The atmosphere hummed with gathering
insects preparing themselves for rain. It was especially hot.
    The first suicide of the season flushed free of the crags that had
held him below the virgin flushing of Victoria Falls. If it didn't rain
soon, there would be more of those. There is nothing like October
in this part of the world to make suicide seem a reasonable option.
    To reach the office where they took my blood, I had to leave the
dusty street and climb up a rusting fire escape to a door that had
once been painted British colonial green: a few green fingernail
chunks of enamel had weathered thirty years of independent Africa.
The door was mostly peeled to red-grey and had been propped open
by the body of a man, still breathing. His flanks shone through a
torn shirt. I negotiated several such bodies—a collapsible queue of
patients—to reach the door from the street: men holding their heads;
women holding babies; children holding babies; women holding their
dignity together in tight cocoons of bright cloth around their knees,
their necks lolling with the weight of their heads.
    The Shona of Zimbabwe have a name for this special way that
African women must sit. The proper way, with legs outstretched and

knees flat. Such an impossible position for knee-crossing, toilet-sitting Westerners. The Shona call this way of sitting *kutambarara*. The elders—those thirty-year-old mothers of eight—had said to their daughters, 'You will meet with profound indignity in your life. You will meet with unspeakable horror. At least know how to sit.' By forty-two, the elders were dead; killed by the almost-inevitability of what they called the Very Disease, or by the tremblings of yellow fever, or by bilharzia lodged in the spine and brain, or by a vague but fatal pain in the chest, or by sheer bloody exhaustion.

In knee-buckling heat the women and girls—students of the elders and themselves approaching motherhood, elder-apprenticeship, at twelve years old—sat with dignity in the face of all the indignities Africa can heap on a woman. And those incapable of propping themselves up melted into a lying-down position, knees still pressed together. Only the babies were dead-frog, legs flopped open, relaxed, unconscious of their bodies. Sometimes unconscious.

The smell that wafted up from the hot metal steps towards me was the fevered scent of cold sweat; peculiarly malarial, woolly and faintly uric. My own sweat, cold on hot skin, added to the aura of humid ill-health. The taste of chronic sickness was a pale coating of bitterness on my tongue. Since the baby was born a vague churning in my stomach combined with the leg-clinging heat to prevent me from eating. I stepped (long legs) over the body of the unflinching man blocking the door and held Sarah tighter to me. She was pink-white and naked, in contrast to everyone else there; protected from the diseases of Africa by my paranoia. I had not stopped holding her since the moment I scooped her from her chicken coop at the clinic in Zimbabwe.

In Africa, the mere act of letting go, even for a moment, seemed enough to snatch life away into air-filled nothing.

Where her skin touched mine there was a thin film of glueing sweat.

In the gloomy hot dim light of the doctor's offices, the receptionist slumped at a wooden desk—an old government-issue school desk—under an open window. A blue cotton curtain had been tied at its waist to allow for more airflow. The air was not complying.

'Excuse me?'

The receptionist lolled and barely lifted her head off the pile of papers on which she had been resting and on which, I noticed, she had left a greasy sweat mark. 'Yes?'

'I need to see the doctor.'

She picked her ear vigorously and looked uninterestedly at the result on the tip of her fingernail. She wiped it off on the pile of papers.

'Please?' I tried.

'But look.' She indicated the door.

I looked out at the long, hot line of patients who, like me, were hoping to see the doctor before he knocked off at five. And I knew that if this were in theory, I should have waited my turn with everybody else.

So I dug in my pocket and handed the woman a thin slice of brown, 500-kwacha notes.

'You or the baby?' She nonchalantly pressed the bribe into the fold in the top of her dress, where it rested above her breast next to the other money she had collected as guard against the inevitability of her own malaria, a funeral expense, a new outfit from the bright flag-like collection of dresses shifting humidly from wires in the second-hand market.

'For me.'

'Is it malaria?'

I shook my head and shrugged Sarah on to my shoulder. 'Yes. Perhaps.' If it wasn't typhoid, typhus, hepatitis, childbirth fever. 'Something more,' I said.

I had already treated myself for malaria, first with chloroquine, then with Halfan and finally with Fansidar, but either I didn't have malaria, or the malaria I had was resistant to all these drugs. Or I was being re-infected almost daily with the parasite and I could never be cured.

Every week we swallowed a deltaprim—a single pill designed as a prophylactic against malaria. We burned mosquito coils under our beds and under the dining-room table and on the floor in the sitting room and around the bed. We wore insect repellent. We slept under mosquito nets. None of these strategies prevented the waves of malaria which afflicted us all. But most of us stayed alive—if thinner and more yellow—until the end of another rainy season.

'Yes,' I told the woman, 'it's that there's something else…'

But the receptionist had fallen back on to her desk with profound uninterest. 'Take a seat,' she told me, her voice muffled by the muggy heap of patients' records and nurses' notes on which she was preparing to resume her siesta.

I didn't take a seat. Instead I stood as close as I could to the window and rocked the pink baby on my shoulder, facing her towards the trees outside and the hot uprise of dust from the street and away from the tiny, germ-jostling room.

Below the waiting-room window, I could see the exuberant purple bloom of the jacaranda trees. Occasionally, the wind lifted the rotting-sweet scent of decomposing petals up to the baby and me. She nuzzled her wobbling, tiny head into my neck and moved her lips, so I dropped her to my waist, buried her under my shirt and let her nurse, rocking on my feet. Waiting.

The inner waiting room, which also appeared to be the examination room, was where we waited after waiting in the outer waiting room and before that on the fire escape. It seemed to have enjoyed a previous identity under colonial rule as a pantry or broom cupboard. The small green windowless box, its walls scarred where shelves must once have been, was now waist-deep in African faces peering up from a single, slim bench and from the floor. The air was thick with breath and sweat, which gently evaporated and filmed the floors and walls with clamminess.

I was here with the lucky few able to see the nurses and then the doctor before they finished for the day and went home to a meal which even as we waited was being prepared over stoves and fires in the pale afternoon heat. In those poor, ground-scraped sections of town, colonial madams had kept elaborate gardens and white-gloved servants thirty years ago, and dinner would have been the too-hot cloying taste of baking meat made palatable only by gin.

The nurse offered me a seat on a bench by dislodging a woman with a small baby, both of whom were half asleep against the wall.

'I can't sit,' I told her.

'You must sit. This lady,' the nurse indicated the recently ousted woman and her startled, wakeful baby, 'can sit on the floor. You can't sit on the floor.'

'No,' I insisted, 'I can't sit.'

'But you will faint if you don't sit.'

Alexandra Fuller

'No I won't.'

The nurse shrugged.

'Tell the lady she can sit on the bench again.' I smiled at the woman on the floor and indicated the bench.

'She's just okay on the floor.'

The woman was sitting bolt upright with legs outstretched but she had closed her eyes and appeared to have gone back to sleep. The baby blinked dark brown eyes at me.

The nurse made me stretch out my arms, which I did one at a time, shuffling Sarah from one hip to the other.

A black enamel pot was boiling weakly on a small electric ring in the corner. The steam added to the humidity in the room. In the pot were syringes and needles jostling in the bubbling water, but I make the nurse open a fresh needle in front of me.

'It will cost extra,' she said.

'Cheaper than a funeral,' I told her.

'Tch, tch.'

'One-in-three,' I reminded her, 'infected with Aids.'

'The Very Disease,' she corrected.

'Why don't you call it what it is?'

'Give me your arm.'

'Fresh needle,' I said again.

'We boil the needles, you can see for yourself. Everybody else uses boiled needles. Do you think you are more special than everybody out there?' She was not being unkind.

'No,' I lied. But I paid my extra 500 kwacha and I watched as the nurse cracked the fresh syringe and needle out of the sterile blue packet and I didn't let my eyes off the needle until it was sunk into the pale blue line in the crook of my arm. The nurse struggled to find a vein. 'You're thirsty.'

I looked away. The baby started to bleat.

'Nice baby,' said the nurse, breathing heavily in my ear. She had started to sweat, and so had I. Our cloud of moisture wafted up and met in a little black storm cloud above our heads. My empty stomach clenched with nausea. The nurse gave up. 'Let's try the other arm.'

'I'm going to drop the baby,' I said. I was taking deep breaths in through a wide mouth, swallowing hot air. Sarah was handed to the other nurse, who took her by the shoulders, sharply swinging her up with casual inelegance. 'Pretty baby,' cooed the other nurse. She frowned at me. 'But she is cold. You must dress her.'

'It's a hundred thousand degrees out there,' I said, holding up a fresh vein for my nurse.

'She'll die of pneumonia.'

'You people put too many clothes on your babies.'

'You people don't put enough.'

'Maybe there are some people in the middle who put just the right amount.'

Then I couldn't talk any more because the now-blunt needle was searching for blood in my other arm.

In the corner of the waiting room a thin young man in a stained white coat was leaning over a microscope—it looked like the kind we used in junior school to look at leaf cells. He was slipping one slide after the other into view. The microscope was balanced on battered, dog-eared books that in turn were propped on an old string-covered bar stool. 'How does he remember which slide is which?'

No one answered me. I guessed that all the slides showed positive malaria results. All the blood's the same here, I thought: malarial, diseased, weak, pale, thin.

The doctor was an Indian, small and dark with the skin at his ears and nose and temple a deep shade of blue. His neck appeared to have been loosened from his shoulders and when he spoke it wobbled, puppet-like.

'Please sit down, Mrs Charlie.'

'I'd rather stand.' I swayed the baby on my shoulder and she spat up warm pools of curdled milk on to the nappy on my shoulder.

'Oh, whatever you wish,' said the doctor, 'yes, yes, whatever.' The whites of his eyes were stained nicotine-yellow. He studied a piece of paper on his desk with some intensity and then suddenly asked, 'How's business for Charlie?'

'Fine.'

I sighed.

The doctor nodded. 'Yes, yes. Of course.' The doctor tapped the piece of paper on his desk and said, 'Very bad. Lots of parasites. You definitely have malaria. Many, many little parasites. Look!' He waved the piece of paper at me as evidence.

Alexandra Fuller

'I know I have malaria.'
'You've tried chloroquine?'
'Chloroquine, Halfan, Fansidar.'
We stared at each other. 'I had the baby,' I said, swivelling my shoulder so he could see Sarah's face.
'Oh, did you? Yes you did.' He looked at the baby, as if suddenly noticing her.
I waited. And then I volunteered, 'Two weeks ago.'
'Nice baby,' he said, eyeing her suspiciously.
'A girl.'
'Well,' his head wobbled, 'too bad, eh? Too bad. Never mind, never mind. Next time a boy, eh?'
I cleared my throat. 'I think,' I told the doctor in a low voice, 'there is a problem from...childbirth.'
'You're very thin,' said the doctor, frowning.
'It's very hot,' I pointed out. 'And I'm sick. Can't eat.'
'Oh, but you must eat.'
'I have malaria.'
'Of course, of course,' the doctor's head wobbled some more, 'everybody and also you.'
'The thing is...it hurts.'
'To eat?'
'No...not to eat. But the...other.'
'The other?'
'Where the baby came out,' I whispered. 'I can't sit down.'
The doctor snapped back in his chair and was jarred into a period of intense neck waggling.
I was close to tears. 'It hurts to sit down. My...bottom.'
His colour deepened, flushing up from the neck, so that he resembled a furious chameleon. 'This is not problem for me,' his voice raised with indignation. 'Very common. Go home, drink water, eat food.'
'But it is a bloody problem.'
'Malaria,' he insisted.
'You don't get malaria in your bottom,' I said.
The doctor frowned and pushed out his lips stubbornly so that they formed a sudden, moist rosebud in his brown face.
'Even I know that,' I said. 'Listen,' I told the doctor, 'something

106

is not okay down there and somebody is going to have to take a look. You're a bloody doctor, aren't you?'

He waved his hand at me, dismissing the idea, refuting the thin, fly-shit-spattered certificate which curled yellowly in a wooden frame above his desk, 'Well…' He was also infamous for kneading the breasts and thighs of American women river guides who passed through. Surely a fleeting glance at my bottom was not outside the realm of his experience.

Nurses were recruited and I was extracted from the inner sanctum of the doctor's office and taken to the outer sanctum of the examination/waiting room. A space was cleared on the floor around the single bed and several reluctant patients were removed from the bed itself. '*Ndalomba! Ndalomba!*' and the patients scrambled off the bed or shuffled back on their haunches. Children, bored by disease and waiting into distant staring, were brought back to proper childish life and curiosity. They peered up at me with interest. Even the dignified women strained above the heads of their babies to look at me. The nurse patted the bed. 'You lie here,' she told me. She tried, without much success, to pull the sagging, clammy curtain around the bed. In the event, the curtain reached neither around the circumference of the wafer-thin bed, nor down (except in exhausted snatches) below the level of the bare mattress. It had shrunk in the humidity.

Sarah had fallen asleep in my arms. Her nappy was hot and warm and soaked through, the sweet smell of her infant urine powerful but not enough to overcome the room's soupy raw-onion fragrance of collective body odour. I climbed on to the bed and nestled her on to my chest where she gave a startled bleat before falling asleep again. Where her thick nappy bulged out of the edges of her plastic pants, pee soaked into my shirt. I hadn't yet developed a mother's habit of carrying enough emergency and non-emergency supplies to clothe and feed a small family for a week.

There was no hospital gown to cover my body and no sheet, disposable or otherwise, to pull up over my knees. I toyed with the idea of facing the wall for some semblance of privacy, but that would have made it hard for the nurses to examine me. So, resigned to the exhibition, I wriggled out of my shorts and exposed my bottom to the nurses and to the sea of frankly fascinated Zambian faces at the

end of the bed. The two nurses took it in turn, handing a torch back
and forth to each other, both reluctant to begin the examination.

'You are very thin,' said one nurse, pressing on my hip bones.

'That's not where it hurts.'

The other nurse tugged my knees open and switched the torch
on. 'Ah,' she said, discarding it with disgust, 'Chinese batteries.
Dead.' She asked me hopefully, 'You don't have a spare battery with
you?'

I shook my head.

She tugged the curtains open for better light. There was a guffaw
from a small boy on the bench who had climbed on to his mother's
lap for a better view.

'You must eat more meat,' the nurse told me.

'I'm a vegetarian.'

'What?'

I was too tired and thirsty and humiliated to begin explaining the
logic of voluntarily rejecting an entire food group on the basis of
environmental and moral philosophies. 'See anything?' I asked. 'Have
the stitches healed?'

'Stitches?'

'They cut me open to get the baby out.'

'Tch, tch. Why cutting?'

'She was too big.'

'You are too little.'

There was more probing from the nurses, more snorts of laughter
from the quickly-recovering malarial patients in the waiting room.
Suddenly one of the nurses gave a shout of recognition. 'Ah,
Madam!' she said, emerging victorious from between my legs,
brandishing the impotent torch, 'You have a bunch of fruits by your
bottom.'

A dozen Zambians showed a less than polite interest in this
development.

'A bunch of what?' I scrambled to a sitting position and pulled
my shorts up, glaring furiously at my audience who quickly averted
their faces.

'You have him-i-rods.'

'Him-i-rods?'

'The fruits of the bottom.'

'Oh, Jesus.' I inched my way carefully off the edge of the bed. I used to laugh at advertisements promoting haemorrhoid relief on television back in my university days overseas. 'Do you ever suffer from the pain and itch of haemorrhoids?' a grey-haired man had asked in polite Canadian tones, holding up a tube of something. Grapes-be-gone perhaps?

The nurse shook her head as if to say, *All that fuss for a few fruits.*

I took Sarah back and asked, 'Is there any treatment? Do you have anything for haemorrhoids?'

The nurses hid their giggling behind hands.

'No, I didn't think so.'

'Take aspirin,' offered one nurse.

'Eat some fat,' observed the other.

'Thank you.'

'Elevate your bottom.'

'Drink milk.'

I left the office. I was enlightened, but in no way relieved, by my hours there. I looked around at the other patients still waiting to see the doctor and considered asking them if anyone had suffered from the 'fruits of the bottom' and if so, how did they cure the pain. Haemorrhoids, I though with some despair, were probably the least of my fellow patients' worries.

When I got home, I delicately lowered myself on to the bed, I sat with legs out in front, knees slightly flexed.

I breathed deeply and waited.

Kutambarara turned out to be the perfect sitting position for a woman suffering from the pain and itch of haemorrhoids. □

GRANTA

NEVER NEVERLAND
Rodrigo Fresán

TRANSLATED FROM THE SPANISH BY
NATASHA WIMMER

J. M. Barrie in 1902.

That old-fashioned boy, that sepia-coloured boy sitting under the walnut table where they've set his brother's coffin, is called James Matthew Barrie, and he's six years old, and he's pretending to hide from a terrible pirate. They won't find him here, he's sure of it, hidden by the skirt of the tablecloth, protected in the ship's hold by the new dead body of David Barrie: the family's great hope, the chosen one, the electrifying light in a home lit by candles.

David Barrie: athletic and handsome and good at school and sure to become a minister, to bask in heavenly and academic glory as an admired Doctor of Divinity; and who will read all those books of philosophy and theology now, who?

'Why him? Why did it have to be him?' weep the women who've come to weep. And the sound of their tears makes James Matthew Barrie think of the treacherous singing of mermaids, of shipwrecked adventurers, of distant shores. James Matthew Barrie isn't very good at sports: short, his head too big for his too-small body. James Matthew Barrie is the constant worry of his teachers, because James Matthew Barrie, tiny James Matthew Barrie, always seems to be somewhere else, somewhere far away. So unlike his brother David they might belong to two different races.

David was, is, and always will be the favourite of his mother, Margaret Ogilvy, who's kept her maiden name according to old tradition and has now retired to her rooms and closed the windows and drawn the curtains so that she won't hear anything or anyone. The constant noise of the looms coming out of all the houses and up the street makes James Matthew Barrie imagine—under the table, playing with his little sister Maggie under David's coffin—that he's hearing the clash of the many blades of many gentlemen fighting simultaneous duels for the heart of a single, unattainable princess. James Matthew Barrie has the rare gift of being able to travel without moving.

Margaret Ogilvy won't rise from her bed, even to deposit a last kiss on the ever bluer lips of her favourite prince. David, the best of her ten children. David, dead in a skating accident just as he was about to turn fourteen, on an icy loch as cold as a mirror, in the Grampian Hills outside of Kirriemuir, in the county of Forfarshire, in Scotland, in the terrible and unforgettable winter of 1867.

Rodrigo Fresán

James Matthew Barrie will immortalize this place in several of his books, calling it the Thrums, the name the inhabitants of Kirriemuir—a town of spinners and looms—have given to the skeins spinning on wooden frames.

And here he is now.

Spinning on his own axis.

James Matthew Barrie (Barrie, from now on) was born on May 9, 1860 and was baptized in the South Free Church the following Sunday as the ninth child of David Barrie and Margaret Ogilvy, who were married at twenty-seven and twenty-one and had seven daughters and three sons. Alexander, the oldest boy, was born in 1841; Mary Edward, the oldest girl, in 1854; Jane Ann Adamson in 1847, David in 1853, Sara in 1854, Isabella in 1857, Margaret in 1863. Elizabeth and Agnes died very early, in their cradles. A good return for the age: just two lives lost out of ten. Mark a cross next to their names in the register, lay them in little pine boxes, cover the boxes with earth, and life goes on; there wasn't even time for them to learn to say their own names. And, thinks Margaret Ogilvy, you don't miss, or don't miss too much, someone you haven't even come to understand.

Margaret Ogilvy doesn't really understand Barrie, the youngest of her sons, very well either. There's something incomplete about him, about the way he looks in the few pictures taken of him as a child; because why bother to photograph a boy who doesn't even seem interesting enough to impress his image forcefully on paper? In his childhood photographs, Barrie always looks imprecise. More like a sketch than a portrait. Closer to the oil painting of an apprentice than to the brand-new and almost automatic miracle of photography's developing fluids. Barrie, always dressed in little suits that try to give some distinction to his small body with its short arms and big feet and enormous head. His moon face crowds as many features into as small a space as possible. It's as if his eyes and nose and mouth seek the exact centre of that pale circle, which always seems to have just emerged from the eclipse of a long and dull and exhausting illness.

In her photographs, on the other hand, Margaret Ogilvy looks firm and strong: a gentle despot, a professional mother, head of the tribe. Her husband occupies himself with affairs outside the house. Her husband is one of the most respected men in the community, and he's known and admired for his business skills. Her husband would never let her children be devoured by the mills, always ravenous for wool; her husband has better plans for those who carry his name. Margaret Ogilvy steers the house like a ship, not letting go of the rudder for a second, her eyes always fixed on the horizon, looking ahead, searching for land. It's hard for me to imagine either of these two—Margaret Ogilvy or David Barrie—telling their children stories. It's hard for me to believe they know any stories.

There are more than noticeable differences between a photograph of Margaret Ogilvy before young David's death and one taken several years after he was brought to his mother on a sled, dead and almost unmarked, his neck broken and bones jumbled nonetheless as if by one of those whirlwinds of dead leaves that come rushing down the Highland rocks. David's eyes are open. I always wondered what it meant, that final choice: dying with eyes open or eyes shut. When a person's eyes are open does it mean that what they saw in the final second of life was too beautiful, or, conversely, when their eyes are shut, does it mean that what they glimpsed on the other side was so terrible that the darkness behind the curtain of their eyelids was preferable?

In the first of the photographs, Margaret Ogilvy is the perfect incarnation of matriarchal power and self-satisfaction. A woman with a mission, her modest but dignified bonnet tied with a bow under her chin. Margaret Ogilvy smiles the smile of someone who feels invulnerable, the winner of wars no one should even bother declaring against her. What would be the point, why fight in retreat without ever having reached the battle? The photograph is out of focus, not because the photographer made a mistake but because it was impossible to keep Margaret Ogilvy still in those days of long exposures. A minute was too much time to waste staring at a wooden box with a glass eye, thought Margaret Ogilvy.

The second of the photographs, from 1871, is a typical studio portrait that shows her with her gaze lost and her skin nearly translucent; she is dressed with great elegance, but Margaret Ogilvy is now a weaker and more fearful woman. A motionless woman. A woman who's had one of the most important chapters ripped from her life story. In this photograph, one hand is raised to her face but doesn't quite touch it, perhaps for fear of not finding it, or even worse, of passing through it as if it were water or air. It's the

Rodrigo Fresán

photograph of a living ghost, of a woman who—beginning January 1867, after 'My son is not dead! My son will never die!', and until her own death twenty-nine years later—has been living on another planet for too many years. The planet David, in the Nebula of the Oldest Son, so near the constellation of the Dead Skater, so far from earth.

Barrie, the author of *Peter Pan*, will say one day that 'nothing that happens to us after we are twelve matters very much,' disguising with this clever exaggeration the lucky shock of the most important thing: the thing that will mark the rest of his days, that happened to him when he was only six years old and had an older brother who'd just died.

Barrie remembers that two telegrams arrived from the office at Forfar. The first brought news of the accident (David hadn't even been skating; a friend was pushing him from behind and David fell and hit his head on the ice); the second told of the tragic outcome.

David is brought on a sled as night falls. He's brought on a sled by coloured men, men recently come from the mills, covered in the red, green, gold and blue of the enormous barrels of dye. It looks, thinks Barrie, like the funeral of a king of the elves. It's trolls that bring David slowly along Brechin Road, in a solemn procession, to the house at Lilybanks in the Tenements, Kirriemuir. A house the same as all the rest: a pitched roof, chimney, windows, a front and a back door, and it's not easy to say which of the two doors is the front door, which is the front of the house.

Barrie's sisters—who aren't sure either—divide into two groups and come out the two doors and begin to howl so that neighbours and family won't mistake the path to grief. Barrie hears them from the little washhouse on the other side of the street, across from his house, where he spends most of the day thinking up plays. Barrie comes out of the little house and encounters the body of his brother, who now seems like a puppet whose strings have been stolen, and yet still wears a smile of surprise that not even his family will be able to smooth away when they prepare the body for the funeral.

Barrie stands on a chair and looks into David's coffin, on the table. Barrie smiles back at David, and doesn't quite understand what's happening. The grown-ups tell him to get down from there, and Barrie crawls under the table so that he won't have to see his mother shouting. If there's anything more terrible than shouting, it's seeing where the shouting comes from: shouting always transforms the people who shout, turns them into something new and terrible; and Barrie doesn't recognize his mother any more, struck as she is by the lightning bolt of her shouting. The windowpanes tremble, outside a dog barks, and someone else shouts too; because stray shouts always find a shout to join.

Barrie's father orders his daughters to take their mother to her room. The daughters—smaller shouts bowing down to the big shout—obey immediately and little Barrie hears them going up the stairs. A shout for each step from oldest to youngest in turn, then back to the beginning. A door opens and a door closes and for the next few days the house seems to hang in the air, as if frozen in a time without motion, as if Margaret Ogilvy's shout has forever altered the mechanisms governing time and space.

Nothing important ever happened in Kirriemuir, but after David's death the only thing that happens in the house on Brechin Road is his death. Over and over again. Settled at the head of the family table, at church, everywhere. Barrie evades this non-event of living death. Barrie escapes by losing himself in books. Barrie opens books like windows, opens books to let the light of a story into his gloomy life. Barrie reads to leave his surroundings behind, and the books become part of him. Barrie and *Robinson Crusoe* and *The Arabian Nights* in a deluxe children's edition, without scandalous illustrations. Barrie reads stories about lone travellers and lost travellers. Barrie imagines his mother as a queen taken prisoner. Barrie enters his mother's bedroom, which is always dark, as if he were venturing into a treasure cave or a storm at sea. He enters books and closes them, and Barrie asks himself what happens when a book closes, when the story it tells is interrupted. Barrie asks himself what the book's speed is: is it the author's speed as he was writing, or is it the speed readers reach as they read? And also: does a book stop when it's left aside or are books perpetual motion machines that work with no need of readers? Books like magic engines that never stop driving their heroes and villains toward new shores and palaces, and that's why it isn't a good idea to interrupt your reading of them, thinks Barrie: you miss so many things when you close a book. There are nights that

Rodrigo Fresán

Barrie could swear he hears the books talking among themselves, mingling, recounting their lives and works, recalling their plots, their best moments. Barrie thinks that reading is the making of memories and that writing is also the making of memories. The memories of the person who writes—the only thing writers do is *remember* something they happened to think of, something that happened to them or never happened to them, but that's happening *now* as they write—are incorporated into the memories of the person who reads until it's impossible to say where the memories of one end and the other begin. The writer as intermediary, as spiritual spirit guide, as elucidator of the way books are the ghosts of living writers, and dead writers are the ghosts of books. And maybe *this* is immortality, never getting old, Barrie says to himself. Ink as the elixir of eternal life, drunk through the eyes, and Barrie thinks that if there's anything better than being a writer, it's being a character.

Barrie thinks about all these things.

Barrie wonders about the meaning of certain illustrations in certain books. Barrie thinks about the happiness we feel when we reach a certain paragraph and understand at last why a chapter's called what it's called.

Barrie thinks about the subtle vibration of everything around us the first time we read a sentence we'll never forget. Barrie thinks about all of this so he won't have to think that now it's time to go up and see how his mother is. Barrie doesn't like to go into that room where the air scarcely moves, where everything drags itself on its knees begging for explanations from an implacable God, God's fury barely disguised by his pious cloak of prayers and rogations.

Margaret Ogilvy is the daughter of a fanatically religious bricklayer, and she was brought up in one of the most puritanical Protestant sects, known as the Auld Lichts, or Old Lights. Her task in the sect was to care for the motherless children, the littlest ones. When she got married, she moved to another kirk, her husband's parish, as specified in the marriage laws: the Free Church, which split from the established Church of Scotland in 1843. This splinter branch had no backing and depended on the generosity of its members, who were more liberal than the Auld Lichts. Even so, Margaret Ogilvy always remained attached—body and soul—to the unswerving faith of her elders, among whom it was preached, 'If a man exists who denies the Holy

Spirit, then that man could not have been created by Him.'

Margaret Ogilvy—destroyed by grief and the shock of her grief—doesn't renounce God, but she does renounce her youngest son. James Matthew is so insignificant compared to David. Even under the ground, David seems more real and present than James Matthew.

And this is what happens to Barrie when he's six years old, the instant that marks his whole life, and, so many years later, will end up sparking the legend of a boy frozen in time. This is the day that Barrie receives and conceives his ten commandments.

'Everything is pure supposition until the age of six,' Barrie will write much later; but he'll always remember this moment perfectly, as if seeing it at the theatre or in a book: the date of his real, second birth. Barrie ascends to the summit where Margaret Ogilvy lies, and descends with the tablets of his law, on which a single command may be read. A changeless voice of stone and its echo that knows only how to count to ten, which is more than enough:

Never grow up.
Never grow up.
Never grow up.
Never grow up.
Never grow up.
Never grow up.
Never grow up.
Never grow up.
Never grow up.
Never grow up.

Barrie climbs the stairs. His older sister Jane Ann has told him that it isn't right the way his mother's forgotten him. 'The living have to be at least as important as the dead,' reasons Jane Ann. Barrie thinks about the story of a night in *The Arabian Nights* that he only read part way through. He wants—needs, yearns—to return to that perilous adventure as fast as he can, so it's best to face this other perilous adventure as fast as he can, he tells himself.

Barrie recalls the episode years later in *Margaret Ogilvy*, his successful memoir about his mother published by Hodder & Stoughton in 1896. It's a book that has more to do with him than his mother, because the subject of *Margaret Ogilvy* is the way Barrie analyses the woman who gave birth to him while evoking his despair at having lost his way back to the Land of Childhood.

Barrie climbs the stairs. First he stops in his bedroom—until recently 'David's bedroom'—and opens one of the wardrobes, taking out one of his older brother's suits and putting it on. The Sunday suit. It's very big on him, but, oddly, it fits him better than his own Sunday suit. David's suit seems the product of an operation by an incompetent surgeon, with scars in the strangest and most unlikely places, he thinks.

Barrie knocks at his mother's door. There's no answer. He opens the door. He goes in. He hears nothing from the bed, but that doesn't matter: he can't see the bed in the dark, the kind of darkness there was in the world before electricity reached everywhere—a *dark* darkness. The light of the sun and the moon and even firelight were different back then, too.

Barrie remembers the bed's place in the room and he goes towards it. Barrie breathes deeply, and maybe he's crying without realizing it. Barrie makes noise. He starts to whistle. It's taken him hours, whole days, to perfectly imitate the way David whistled. The cheerful tunes that were always on David's lips as he buried his hands in the pockets of his trousers and strode around the sitting room digging the heels of his boots into the scuffed wooden floor.

This is how Barrie moves now: hopping in the dark, dancing badly like bad dancers, who, as they dance badly, think constantly 'I'm dancing... I'm dancing...' This is how Barrie dances and this is how Barrie whistles and Barrie closes his eyes because he can't see anything anyway.

Then he hears a voice and a question. 'Is that you?' asks his mother. Barrie understands—with the terrible logic of children, logic that's lost as the years go by—that Margaret Ogilvy has confused him with his dead brother. Barrie doesn't answer right away. First he says 'Yes.' After all, she's asking him if he's *him*, and, yes, Barrie *is* Barrie. He hasn't lied, he hasn't sinned. Barrie hears a surprised intake of breath and—this is what scares him most—the beginning of a laugh. It's been a long time since Margaret Ogilvy laughed, and what comes from her throat seems to Barrie more like the cawing of a crow that's been lost for years and finally returns to its nest. There's something mad in that laugh. It's the laugh of someone who's sure that the dead don't die but instead are trapped in an instant, forever unscathed and free from the dictates of the body and the passage of time. It's the laugh of someone who believes in ghosts that never grow old and in dead bodies that don't rot. Barrie can't help being proud to feel, for the first time in his life, that he's an indispensable part of something important and extraordinary. Suddenly, the darkness seems a strange form of light.

'Yes, it's me,' says Barrie happily, and his mother reaches for him and finds him and hugs him. What Barrie feels first is the force of love in the arms that clasp him, and then immediately a powerful disillusion as they let go of him and push him away. Margaret Ogilvy lets out a long, sad moan, like the wind that blows on winter afternoons over the crests of the Grampian hills, and buries her face in the pillow.

'No, no, I'm not him; it's just me,' says Barrie, and he leaves the room and shuts the door, and the pain lasts the exact time it takes him to run down the stairs and open a book to see the footprint left in the sand of a deserted beach, or the wake of a flying carpet in the golden skies of Baghdad, or the gleam of gold in a chest. He doesn't care. He isn't sure. For once, the letters are only letters. Black symbols on white paper that seem to have lost their ability to combine and make stories. Sinbad and Man Friday are no more than creatures of black, leaden blood, men of dry ink. Nothing like what he's just discovered he can become: a cannibal aristocrat. One of those hybrid Eastern beasts the sultans fight. A corsair of make-believe. A writer and a character living inside the same name. Yes: Barrie has discovered his ability not to call up ghosts but to be a ghost himself, and—most important of all—he's had the revelation that those who are loved best are and always will be those who never grow old, who never grow up.

Ghosts, the dead.

The dead who in time become ideals rewritten by the living. The dead are—always—masterpieces of literature. Phantasmagoric fictions, true; but fictions of the kind that manage to survive and surpass any fleshly reality. The dead don't get older but they do expand: like a gas, a poison, a perfume.

'I won't grow up,' swears Barrie.

And he closes the book and opens all the windows in the house.

☐

New Issue – Out Now
_____ Teenage mothers and their newborns.
Portraits from Germany by Annet van der Voort
_____ Why Bhopal is worth remembering 20 years
after the chemical cloud descended by John Vidal
_____ Patrick Brown on the trail of the animal
traffikers in Bangkok and Burma
_____ Tomas Munita treks across the plains with
the nomads of Changpa, India
_____ The New Republic – Chris Morris exposes the
sinister side of nationalism in the Bush White House
_____ PLUS many more exciting, new photo stories,
book reviews, essays and resources

photo: Mothers in Darfur, Sudan by Pierre Abensur fromVol.3 No.3

GRANTA

LILY
Ian McEwan

Lily

Clean and scented, with a dull, near pleasurable ache in his limbs, driving west in light traffic, Henry Perowne, a neurosurgeon, finds he's feeling better about seeing his mother. He knows the routine well enough. Once they're established together, face to face, with their cups of dark brown tea, the tragedy of her situation will be obscured behind the banality of detail, of managing the suffocating minutes, of inattentive listening. Being with her isn't so difficult. The hard part is when he comes away, before this visit merges in memory with all the rest, when the woman she once was haunts him as he stands by the front door and leans down to kiss her goodbye. That's when he feels he's betraying her, leaving her behind in her shrunken life, sneaking away to the riches, the secret hoard of his own existence. Despite the guilt, he can't deny the little lift he feels, the lightness in his step when he turns his back and walks away from the old people's place and takes his car keys from his pocket and embraces the freedoms that can't be hers. Everything she has now fits into her tiny room. And she hardly possesses the room because she's incapable of finding it unaided, or even of knowing that she has one. And when she is in it, she doesn't recognize her things. It's no longer possible to bring her home or take her on excursions; a small journey disorientates or even terrifies her. She has to remain behind, and naturally she doesn't understand that either.

But the thought of the leave-taking ahead doesn't trouble him now. His hour on the squash court means that he's at last suffused with the mild euphoria that follows exercise. That blessed self-made opiate, beta-endorphin smothering every kind of pain. There's a merry Scarlatti harpsichord on the radio tinkling through a progression of chords that never quite resolve, seeming to lead him on towards a playfully receding destination. Along this stretch, where the Euston becomes the Marylebone Road, the traffic signals are phased, Manhattan-style, and he's wafted forwards on a leading edge of green lights, a surfer on a perfect wave of simple information: go! Or even, yes! The long line of tourists—teenagers mostly—outside Madame Tussaud's seems less futile than usual; a generation raised on thunderous Hollywood effects still longs to stand and gawp at waxworks, like eighteenth-century peasants at a country fair. The reviled Westway, rearing on stained concrete piles and on which he rises swiftly to second floor level, offers up a sudden horizon of tumbling cloud above a tumult of rooftops.

125

Ian McEwan

It's one of those moments when to be a car owner in a city, the owner of this car, is sweet. For the first time in weeks, he's in fourth gear. Perhaps he'll make fifth. A sign on a gantry above the traffic-lanes proclaims THE WEST, THE NORTH, as though there lies, spread beyond the suburbs, a whole continent, and the promise of a six day journey.

For almost half a mile he alone possesses this stretch of elevated road. For seconds on end he thinks he grasps the vision of its creators—a purer world that favours machines rather than people. A rectilinear curve sweeps him past recent office buildings of glass and steel, where the lights are already on in the February early afternoon. He glimpses people as neat as architectural models, at their desks, before their screens, even on a Saturday. This is the tidy future of his childhood science fiction comics, of men and women with tight-fitting collarless jumpsuits—no pockets, trailing laces or untucked shirts—living a life beyond litter and confusion, free of clutter fighting evil.

But from a vantage point on the White City flyover, just before the road comes down to earth among rows of red-brick housing, he sees the tail lights massing ahead and begins to brake. His mother never minded traffic lights and long delays. Only a year ago she was still well enough—forgetful, vague, but not terrified—to enjoy being driven around the streets of west London. The lights gave her an opportunity to examine other drivers and their passengers. 'Look at him. He's got a spotty face.' Or simply to say companionably, 'Red again!'

She was a woman who gave her life to housework, to the kind of daily routines of polishing, dusting, vacuuming and tidying that were once common, and these days are only undertaken by patients with obsessive-compulsive disorders. Every day, while Henry was at school, she deep-cleaned her house. She drew her deepest satisfactions from a tray of well-roasted beef, the sheen on a nest of tables, a pile of ironed candy-striped sheets folded in smooth slabs, a larder of neat provisions; or from one more knitted matinee jacket for one more baby in the remoter reaches of the family. The invisible sides, the obverse, the underneath and the insides of everything was clean. The oven and its racks were scrubbed after every use. Order and cleanliness were the outward expression of an unspoken ideal of love. A book he was reading would be back on the hallway shelf upstairs as soon as he put it aside. The morning paper could be in

Lily

the dustbin by lunchtime. The empty milk bottles she put out for collection were as clean as her cutlery. To every item its drawer or shelf or hook, including her various aprons, and her yellow rubber gloves held by a clothes peg, hanging near the egg-shaped eggtimer.

Surely it was because of her that Perowne feels at home in an operating theatre. She too would have liked the waxed black floor, the instruments of surgical steel arrayed in parallel rows on a sterile tray, and the scrub room with its devotional routines—she would have admired the niceties, the clean head-wear, the short fingernails. He should have had her in while she was still capable. It never crossed his mind. It never occurred to him that his work, his fifteen years' training, had anything to do with what she did.

Nor did it occur to her. He barely knew it at the time, but he grew up thinking her intelligence was limited. He used to think she was without curiosity. But that wasn't right. She liked a good exploratory heart-to-heart with her neighbours. The eight-year-old Henry liked to flop on the floor behind the furniture and listen in. Illness and operations were important subjects, especially those associated with childbirth. That was when he first heard the phrase 'under the knife' as well as 'under the doctor'. 'What the doctor said' was a powerful invocation. This eavesdropping may have set Henry on his career. Then there were running accounts of infidelities, or rumours of them, and ungrateful children, and the unreasonableness of the old, and what someone's parent left in a will, and how a certain nice girl couldn't find a decent husband. Good people had to be sifted from the bad, and it wasn't always easy to tell at first which was which. Indifferently, illness struck the good as well as the bad. Later, when he made his dutiful attempts on his daughter Daisy's undergraduate course in the nineteenth-century novel, he recognized all his mother's themes. There was nothing small-minded about her interests. Jane Austen and George Eliot shared them too. Lilian Perowne wasn't stupid or trivial, her life wasn't unfortunate, and he had no business as a young man being condescending towards her. But it's too late for apologies now. Unlike in Daisy's novels, moments of precise reckoning are rare in real life; questions of misinterpretation are not often resolved. Nor do they remain pressingly unresolved. They simply fade. People don't remember clearly, or they die, or the questions die and new ones take their place.

Besides, Lily had another life that no one could have predicted then or remotely guess at now. She was a swimmer. On Sunday morning, September 3, 1939 while Chamberlain was announcing in his radio broadcast from Downing Street that the country was at war with Germany, the fourteen-year-old Lily was at a municipal pool near Wembley, having her first lesson with a sixty-year-old international athlete who had swum for Britain in the Stockholm Olympics in 1912—the first ever women's swimming event. She had spotted Lily in the pool and offered to give her lessons for free, and coached her in the crawl, a most unladylike stroke. Lily went in for local matches in the late Forties. In 1954 she swam for Middlesex in the county championships. She came second, and her tiny silver medal, set in a wooden shield made of oak, always stood on the mantelpiece while Henry was growing up. It's on a shelf in her room now. That silver was as far, or as high, as she got, but she always swam beautifully, fast enough to push out in front of her a deep and sinuous bow wave.

She taught Henry, of course, but his treasured memory of her swimming was of when he was ten, on a school visit one morning to the local pool. He and his friends were changed and ready, had been through the shower and foot-bath, and had to wait on the tiles for the adult session to end. Two teachers stood by, shushing and fussing, trying to contain the children's excitement. Soon there was only one figure remaining in the pool, one in a white rubber cap with a frieze of petals he should have recognized earlier. His whole class was admiring her speed as she surged up the lane, the furrow in the water she left behind, just at the small of her back, and the way she turned her head to breathe without breaking her line in the water. When he knew it was her, he convinced himself he'd known from the beginning. To add to his exaltation, he didn't even have to claim her out loud. Someone called out, 'That's Mrs Perowne!' In silence they watched as she reached the end of her lane right at their feet and performed a flashy underwater turn that was novel at the time. This was no mere duster of sideboards. He'd seen her swim often enough, but this was entirely different; all his friends were there to witness her superhuman nature, in which he shared. Surely she knew, and put on in the last half length a show of demonic speed just for him. Her feet churned, her slender white arms rose and chopped at the water, her bow wave swelled, the furrow deepened. Her body shaped itself round her own wave in a shallow undulating S. You would have had to sprint along the pool to keep up with her. She stopped at the far end and stood, and put her hands on the edge and flipped herself out of the water. She would have been about forty then. She sat there, feet still immersed, pulled off her cap and, tilting her head, smiled shyly in their direction. One of the teachers led the kids into solemn applause. Though it was 1966—the boys' hair was growing thickly over their ears, the girls wore jeans to class—a degree of Fifties formality still prevailed. Henry clapped with the rest, but when his friends gathered round, he was too choked up with pride, too exhilarated to answer their questions, and was relieved to get in the pool where he could conceal his feelings.

In the Twenties and Thirties, great tracts of agricultural land to the west of London disappeared before an onslaught of high-speed housing development, and even now the streets of frowning, respectable two-storey houses haven't quite shaken off their air of suddenness. Each near-identical house has an uneasy, provisional look, as if it knows how readily the land would revert to cereal crops and grazing. Lily now lives only a few minutes away from their old home in Perivale. Henry likes to think that in the misty landscape of her dementia, a sense of familiarity breaks through occasionally and reassures her. By the standards of old people's homes, Suffolk Place is minute—three houses have been knocked through to make one, and an annexe has been added. Out front, privet hedges still mark the old garden boundaries and two laburnum trees survive. One of the three front gardens has been cemented over to make a parking space for two cars. The oversized dustbins behind a lattice fence are the only institutional clues.

Perowne parks and takes the potted plant from the back seat. He pauses a moment before ringing the bell—there's a taste in the air, sweet and vaguely antiseptic that reminds him of his teenage years in these streets, and of a general state of longing, a hunger for life to begin that from this distance seems like happiness. As usual, Jenny opens the door. She's a large, cheerful Irish girl in a blue gingham housecoat who's due to start nurse's training in September. Henry receives special consideration on account of his medical connection—an extra three tea bags in the brew she'll bring soon to his mother's room, and perhaps a plate of chocolate fingers. Without knowing much at all about each other, they've settled on teasing forms of address.

Ian McEwan

'If it isn't the good doctor!'

'How's my fair colleen?'

Off the narrow space of the suburban hallway tinted yellow by the front door's leaded glass is a kitchen of fluorescent light and stainless steel. From there comes a clammy aroma of the lunch the residents ate two hours earlier. After a lifetime's exposure, Perowne has a mild fondness, or at least a complete lack of disgust for institutional food. On the other side of the entrance hall is a narrower door that leads through into the three interconnecting sitting-rooms of the three houses. He can hear the bottled sound of televisions in other rooms.

'She's waiting for you,' Jenny says. They both know this to be a neurological impossibility. Even boredom is beyond his mother's reach.

He pushes the door open and goes through. She is right in front of him, sitting on a wooden chair at a round table covered with a chenille cloth. There's a window at her back, and beyond it, a window of the house next door, ten feet away. There are other women ranged around the edges of the room sitting in high-backed chairs with curved wooden arms. Some are watching, or looking in the direction of, the television mounted on the wall, out of reach. Others are staring in front of them. They stir or seem to sway as he enters, as if gently buffeted by the air the door displaces. There's a general, cheery response to his 'good afternoon, ladies' and they watch him with interest. At this stage they can't be sure he isn't one of their own close relatives. To his right, in the farthest of the connecting sitting-rooms, is Annie, a woman with wild grey hair which radiates from her head in fluffy spokes. She's shuffling unsupported towards him at speed. When she reaches the end of the third sitting room she'll turn back, and keep moving back and forwards all day until she's guided towards a meal, or bed.

His mother is watching him closely, pleased and anxious all at once. She thinks she knows his face—he might be the doctor, or the odd-job man. She's waiting for a cue. He kneels by her chair and takes her hand, which is smooth and dry and very light.

'Hello Mum, Lily. It's Henry, your son Henry.'

'Hello, darling. Where are you going?'

'I've come to see you. We'll go and sit in your room.'

Lily

'I'm sorry, dear. I don't have a room. I'm waiting to go home. I'm getting the bus.'

It pains him whenever she says that, even though he knows she's referring to her childhood home where she thinks her mother is waiting for her. He kisses her cheek and helps her out of her chair, feeling the tremors of effort or nervousness in her arms. As always, in the first dismaying moments of seeing her again, his eyes prick.

She protests feebly. 'I don't know where we can go.'

He dislikes speaking with the forced cheerfulness nurses use on the wards, even on adult patients with no mental impairment. *Just pop this in your mouth for me.* But he does it anyway, partly to disguise his feelings. 'You've got a lovely little room. As soon as you see it, you'll remember. This way now.'

Arm in arm, they walk slowly through the other sitting rooms, standing aside to let Annie pass. It's reassuring that Lily is decently dressed. The helpers knew he was coming. She wears a deep-red skirt with a matching brushed-cotton blouse, black tights and black leather shoes. She always dressed well. Hers must have been the last generation to care as a matter of course about hats. There used to be dark rows of them, almost identical, on the top shelf of her wardrobe, cocooned in a whiff of mothball.

When they step out into a corridor, she turns away to her left and he has to put his hand on her narrow shoulder to guide her back. 'Here it is. Do you recognize your door?'

'I've never been out this way before.'

He opens her door and hands her in. The room is about eight feet by ten, with a glazed door giving on to a small back garden. The single bed is covered by a floral eiderdown and various soft toys that were part of her life long before her illness. Some of her remaining ornaments—a robin on a log, two comically exaggerated glass squirrels—are in a glazed corner-cupboard. Others are ranged about a sideboard close to the door. On the wall near the hand basin is a framed photograph of Lily and Jack, Henry's father, standing on a lawn. Just in shot is the handle of a pram, presumably in which lies the oblivious Henry. She's pretty in a white summer dress and has her head cocked in that shy, quizzical way he remembers well. The young man is smoking a cigarette and wears a blazer and open-necked white shirt. He's tall, with a stoop, and has big hands like his son. His grin is wide and untroubled. It's always useful to have solid proof that the old have had their go at being young. But there is also an element of derision in photography. The couple appear vulnerable, easily mocked for appearing not to know that their youth is merely an episode, or that the tasty smouldering item in Jack's right hand will contribute—Henry's theory—later that same year to his sudden death.

Having failed to remember its existence, Lily isn't surprised to find herself in her room. She instantly forgets that she didn't know about it. However, she dithers, uncertain of where she should sit. Henry shows her into her high-backed chair by the french window, and sits facing her on the edge of the bed. It's ferociously hot. Perhaps his blood is still stirred by the squash game, and the hot shower that followed and the warmth of the car. He'd be content to stretch out on the over-sprung bed and start to think about the day, and perhaps doze a little. How interesting his life suddenly appears from the confines of this room. At that moment, with the eiderdown beneath him, and the heat, he feels a heaviness in his eyes and can't stop them closing. And his visit has hardly begun. To revive himself, he pulls off his sweater, then he shows Lily the plant he has brought.

'Look,' he says. 'It's an orchid for your room.'

As he holds it out towards her, and the frail white flower bobs between them, she recoils.

'Why have you got that?'

'It's yours. It'll keep flowering through the winter. Isn't it pretty? It's for you.'

'It's not mine,' Lily says firmly. 'I've never seen it before.'

He had the same baffling conversation last time. The disease proceeds by tiny unnoticed strokes in small blood vessels in the brain. Cumulatively, the infarcts cause cognitive decline by disrupting the neural nets. She unravels in little steps. Now she's lost her grasp of the concept of a gift, and with it, the pleasure. Adopting again the tone of the cheerful nurse, he says, 'I'll put it up here where you can see it.'

She's about to protest, but her attention wanders. She has seen some decorative china pieces on a display shelf above her bed, right behind her son. Her mood is suddenly conciliatory.

'I've got plenty of them cups and saucers. So I can always go out with one of them. But the thing is, the space between people is so tiny'—she brings up two wavering hands to show him a gap—'that there's hardly enough space to squeeze through. There's too much binding.'

'I agree,' Henry says as he settles back on the bed. 'There's far too much binding.'

Damage from the small-vessel clotting tends to accumulate in the white matter and destroy the mind's connectivity. Along the way, well before the process is complete, Lily is able to deliver her rambling treatises, her nonsense monologues, with touching seriousness. She doesn't doubt herself at all. Nor does she think that he's unable to follow her. The structure of her sentences is intact, and the moods which inflect her various descriptions make sense. It pleases her if he nods and smiles, and chimes in from time to time.

She isn't looking at him as she gathers her thoughts, but past him, concentrating on an elusive matter, staring as though through a window at an unbounded view. She goes to speak, but remains silent. Her pale green eyes, sunk deep in bowls of finely folded light brown skin, have a flat, dulled quality, like dusty stones under glass. They give an accurate impression of understanding nothing. He can't bring her news of the family—the mention of strange names, any names, can alarm her. So although she won't understand, he often talks to her about work. What she warms to is the sound, the emotional tone of a friendly conversation.

He is about to describe to her a patient, the Chapman girl, and how well she's come through, when Lily suddenly speaks up. Her mood is anxious, even a little querulous. 'And you know that this…you know, Aunty, what people put on their shoes to make them…you know?'

'Shoe polish?' He never understands why she calls him Aunty, or which of her many aunts is haunting her.

'No, no. They put it all over their shoes and rub it with a cloth. Well, anyway, it's a bit like shoe polish. It's that sort of thing. We had side plates and God knows what, all along the street. We had everything but the right thing because we were in the wrong place.'

Then she suddenly laughs. It's become clearer to her.

'If you turn the picture round and take the back off like I did you get such a lot of pleasure out of it. It's all what it meant. And the laugh we had out of it!'

And she laughs gaily, just like she used to, and he laughs too. It's all what it meant. Now she's away, describing what might be a disintegrated memory of a street party, and a little water colour she once bought in a jumble sale.

Some time later, when Jenny arrives with the refreshments, Lily stares at her without recognition. Perowne stands and clears space on a low table. He notices the suspicion Lily is showing towards what she takes to be a complete stranger, and so, as soon as Jenny leaves, and before Lily can speak, he says, 'What a lovely girl she is. Always helpful.'

'She's marvellous,' Lily agrees.

The memory of whoever was in the room is already fading. His emotional cue is irresistible and she immediately smiles and begins to elaborate while he spoons all six tea bags out of the metal pot.

'She always comes running, even if it's narrow all the way down. She wants to come on one of them long things but she doesn't have the fare. I sent her the money, but she doesn't have it in her hand. She wants some music, and I said you might as well make up a little band and play it yourself. I worry about her though. I said to her, why do you put all the slices in one bowl when no one's standing up? You can't do it yourself.'

He knows who she's talking about, and waits for more. Then he says, 'You should go and see her.'

It's a long time since he last tried to explain to her that her mother died in 1970. It is easier now to support the delusion and keep the conversation moving along. Everything belongs in the present. His immediate concern is to prevent her eating a tea bag, the way she almost did last time. He piles them onto a saucer which he places on the floor by his foot. He puts a half filled cup within her reach and offers her a biscuit and a napkin. She spreads it over her lap and carefully places the biscuit in its centre. She raises the cup to her lips and drinks. At moments like these—when she's skilful in the long established routines, and looks demure in her colour-matched clothes, a perfectly well-looking seventy-seven-year-old with amazing legs for her age, athlete's legs—he can imagine that it's all been a mistake, a bad dream, and that she'll leave her tiny room and come away with him into the heart of the city and eat fish stew with her daughter-in-law and grandchildren and stay a while.

Lily

Lily says, 'I was there last week, Aunty, on the bus and my mum was in the garden. I said to her, you can walk down there, see what you're going to get, and the next thing is the balancing of everything you've got. She's not well. Her feet. I'll go there in a minute and I can't help losing her a jersey.'

How strange it would have been for Lily's mother, an aloof, unmaternal woman, to have known that the little girl at her skirts would one day, in a remote future, a science fiction date in the next century, talk of her all the time and long to be home with her. Would that have softened her?

Now Lily is set, she'll talk on for as long as he sits there. It's hard to tell if she's actually happy. Sometimes she laughs, at others she describes shadowy disputes and grievances, and her voice becomes indignant. In many of the situations she conjures, she's remonstrating with a man who won't see sense.

'I told him anything that's going for a liberty and he said, I don't care. You can give it away, and I said don't let it waste in the fire. And all the new stuff that's going to be picked up.'

If she becomes too agitated by the story she's telling, Henry will cut in and laugh loudly and say, 'Mum, that's really very funny!' Being suggestible, she'll laugh too and her mood will shift, and the story she tells then will be happier. For now, she's in neutral mode—there's a clock, and a jersey again, and again, a space too narrow to pass through—and Henry, sipping the thick brown tea, half listening, half asleep in the small room's airless warmth, thinks how in thirty-five years or less it could be him, stripped of everything he does and owns, a shrivelled figure meandering in front of his children, while they wait to leave and return to a life of which he'll have no comprehension. High blood pressure is one good predictor of strokes. A hundred and twenty-two over sixty-five last time. The systolic could be lower. Total cholesterol, five point two. Not good enough. Elevated levels of lipoprotein(a) are said to have a robust association with multi infarct dementia. He'll eat no more eggs, and have only semi-skimmed milk in his coffee, and coffee too will have to go one day. He isn't ready to die, and nor is he ready to half die. He wants his prodigiously connected myelin-rich white matter intact, like an unsullied snowfield. No cheese then. He'll be ruthless with himself in his pursuit of boundless health to avoid his mother's fate: Mental death.

'I put sap in the clock,' she's telling him, 'to make it moist.'

An hour passes, and then he forces himself fully awake and stands up, too quickly perhaps, because he feels a sudden dizziness. Not a good sign. He extends both hands towards her, feeling immense and unstable as he looms over her tiny form.

'Come on now, Mum,' he says gently. 'It's time for me to go. And I'd like you to see me to the door.'

Childlike in her obedience, she takes his hands and he helps her from her chair. He piles up the tray and puts it outside the room, then remembers the tea bags, half concealed under the bed, and puts them out too. She might have feasted on them. He guides her into the corridor, reassuring her all the while, aware that she's stepping into an alien world. She has no idea which way to turn as they leave her room. She doesn't comment on the unfamiliar surroundings, but she grips his hand tighter. In the first of the sitting rooms two women, one with snowy hair in braids, the other completely bald, are watching television with the sound off. Approaching from the middle room is Cyril, as always in cravat and sports jacket, and today carrying a cane and wearing a deerstalker. He's the home's resident gent, sweet-mannered, marooned in one particular, well-defined fantasy: he believes he owns a large estate and is obliged to go around visiting his tenants and be scrupulously polite. Perowne has never seen him unhappy.

Cyril raises his hat at Lily and calls. 'Good morning, my dear. Everything well? Any complaints?'

Her face tightens and she looks away. Then she is suddenly agitated and trying to tell Henry something important.

'If it gets too dry it will curl up again. I told him, and I told him you have to water it, but he wouldn't put it down.'

'It's all right,' he tells her. 'He will put it down. I'll tell him to. I promise you.'

He needs to concentrate on his leave-taking, for he knows that she'll think she's coming with him. He'll be standing once more at the front door, with his meaningless explanation that he'll return soon. Jenny or one of the other girls will have to distract her as he steps outside.

Together they walk back through the first sitting-room. Tea and crustless sandwiches are being served to the ladies at the round table with the chenille cloth. He calls a greeting to them, but they seem too distracted to reply. Lily is happier now, and leans her head against his arm. As they come into the hall they see Jenny Lavin by the door, already raising her hand to the high double security lock and smiling in their direction. Just then his mother pats his hand with a feathery touch and says, 'Out here it only looks like a garden, Aunty, but it's the countryside really and you can go for miles. When you walk here you feel lifted up, right high across the counter. I can't manage all them plates without a brush, but God will take care of you and see what you're going to get because it's a swimming race. You'll squeeze through somehow.' ☐

remembering brodsky

artist's book
edition of 20
25 images · ewa monika zebrowski
endnote · mark strand
US$750 ezebrowski@hotmail.com

fondamenta degli incurabili, detail, 2003 © ewa m. zebrowski

GRANTA

MUTATIONS
Masha Gessen

Mutations

I spent the day of August 21, 1992, driving to a mountainous desert town whose name, in the scorching heat and fine dust, was a seductive mockery: Palm Springs, California. It was the most Californian of endeavours, an editorial retreat for the Los Angeles-based magazine where I worked. I ate dinner with my colleagues at a bland Mexican restaurant. I had two sour margaritas, talked more than I usually did, and told a story that left me vaguely uneasy, as I always feel when I talk about my mother: I cannot talk about her without telling lies. I don't remember what I said, but it was something complimentary, even prideful, I think, and though I loved my mother and was proud of her, talking of her in that way, with all that had gone wrong between us, was most certainly a lie.

I woke up at four that morning, in the bedroom of a rental bungalow, with a wave of nausea pushing its way up to my burning dry throat. I stumbled to the bathroom and threw cold water inside and on myself, washing my face and head clumsily, then looked at my bloated face in the mirror and wondered how two margaritas could have done this to me. I went back to bed and next opened my eyes at a few minutes before seven, without a trace of a hangover but with a sudden wakefulness I could not fight. With hours to kill before the meetings began, I tried going out for a walk in the desolation of Palm Springs, considered a swim in the kidney-shaped pool, and finally went back inside the bungalow intending to read some magazine submissions. I spread them out on the coffee table and, before starting, picked up the phone and dialled my parents in Boston. I was checking in at least daily back then and knew they'd be awake—they were three hours ahead. These considerations were background noise; I'd picked up the phone without pausing to think, and was just getting one of my daily chores out of the way while I was killing time.

A strange male voice answered the phone. 'Papa?' I asked, knowing that it wasn't.

'Hold a minute,' the man said nervously, and a moment later my father came on the line. My mother was dead. The man answering the phone was a policeman who had come to fill out a report which, as it turned out, is a necessary part of letting someone die at home.

My mother had been diagnosed with breast cancer two years earlier. By the following summer, it had already spread to her bones, and six

JOSE MANUEL NAVIA/NETWORK PHOTOGRAPHERS

141

months before she died she was told it may be in her liver—it wasn't then, but it got there and killed her.

My mother had last woken up at seven that morning—four o'clock in California, when I'd first woken up—and asked for ice cream. Her liver was failing. Her throat must have been burning up. She died a few minutes before ten. That was the moment I had bolted awake for the second time, the bizarre toxic symptoms of three hours earlier mysteriously gone, and my inextricable physical relationship to my mother proven to me for the first time in my conscious life—at the very moment hers ended.

The second time the physical relationship proved itself was on January 28, 2004, at a coffee bar in Cambridge, Massachusetts—an accidental location I'll avoid in the future, much as I have avoided revisiting Palm Springs. I was sitting at a small square table, trying to fix my ailing laptop, when my cellphone rang and a professionally sensitive woman's voice said, 'I am returning your call. Yes, the results of your tests have arrived. And there is a change.' She paused. 'In the BRCA1 gene, there is a deleterious mutation.' She paused. 'I'm sorry.'

She was calling to say that my mother had passed on the bad gene, the breast cancer gene (that's what BRCA stands for, a scientific abbreviation that is too easy to decipher: breast cancer). I was surprised. I was shocked. I shouldn't have been. I had gone to get tested, I had known enough to know that I was a likely candidate for the mutation, but I was convinced that I was negative. Even if my mother had been a carrier—I couldn't know, because she died two years before the gene was discovered—I had only a fifty per cent chance of having inherited it. That night in Palm Springs had taught me nothing: I was certain I was immune to my mother's physical legacy.

Something had gone wrong between me and my mother, something so profound and so old that I find it difficult to describe. There was no tragic fight, no horrible misunderstanding. For as long as I can remember, we simply felt like strangers, not particularly intimate ones except by virtue of circumstance: we happened to live together. Nothing between us was ever unconditional, even the physical proximity. I left home at fifteen.

Our relationship was a frozen sea, with scattered tiny islands of common ground. She died before we'd had much chance to claim those islands: before I wrote anything she—also a writer and a translator—would have enjoyed reading, before I translated my first book, using what I had learned from watching her work, and before I too became a mother.

When I started writing professionally, she said proudly, 'My genes have won out.' I remember being surprised, and silently dissenting: I did not doubt my mother's gifts, but I never believed they were also mine. I counted on more—and less. My mother was a more talented writer, a more diligent reader and a more enterprising student. She was also handicapped by a desperate fear of people that could turn routine communication into a feat of heroism. She died at forty-nine, still gifted but not accomplished: even if by external measure she may have been considered successful, she still felt anonymous and overlooked. I think that long-ago conversation with my colleagues in Palm Springs had in fact concerned my mother's career achievements, and this was why it had left me so uneasy. I know the fear too, but of necessity I learned to get out and make my way among people early, and I had always thought that this was why I had done well with barely half of her gifts. I had assumed I was simply better at living than she had been. And even though, like all daughters of mothers who die young, I have a difficult time visualizing myself past a certain age, I had always, without really thinking about it, assumed that I would make better of what I had, and for longer, because I am not as afraid. I thought my gifts were my own, making me free from her legacy altogether. Then I found out that I got everything from her, including the flaw that killed her.

Here is the story of my flaw. I carry a genetic mutation that kills women early—earlier and earlier with each generation—through breast and ovarian cancer. Scientists have identified two genes (BRCA1 and BRCA2) as influencing these cancers. If these genes are damaged in certain known ways (two ways are known for BRCA1 and one for BRCA2), a woman's risk of breast and ovarian cancer increases manifold. The hereditary roulette works as follows. All of us have two copies of each and every gene. Those with the mutation have one normal copy and one damaged one. A child inherits one copy of every gene from each parent, so if one parent has a mutation, the child has a fifty per cent chance of getting a damaged copy of the gene. That, in turn, in the case of the BRCA gene means that her lifetime risk of breast cancer may be as high as eighty-five per cent, and the risk of ovarian cancer may go up to fifty per cent. For some reason, probably having to do with the environment or diet or lifestyle, these days women with the mutation are getting the cancers at an earlier age than their mothers' and grandmothers' generations.

From what we know about genes, the bad ones are supposed to get washed out of the population through natural selection. No one knows for certain why some mutations survive, but the theory many scientists subscribe to is that, in addition to causing disease, they serve a protective function against other, more common ailments. The effect of the sickle-cell anaemia gene, for example, is known to be protective against malaria. The Tay-Sachs gene, some believe, may guard against tuberculosis. These genetic mutations can perform their protective function if the carrier has just one copy of the gene with a mutation; they cause disease only if a child inherits the 'bad' gene from both mother and father—a twenty-five per cent probability when the parents are carriers. There are critics of these theories, those who say that talk of natural selection in a modern population of humans is highly suspect, but it's a way to understand how genetic mutations get passed on through generations.

The story of the breast-and-ovarian-cancer mutations is more harsh. There is no indication that these mutations have any sort of protective effect. If a foetus inherits two bad copies of a BRCA gene—one from each parent—it will not be viable. A girl baby who is born with only one defective copy of the gene will not develop cancer as long as the other copy is functioning. But when the 'good' copy also suffers a mutation—as, it seems, will happen in most cases—cancer will develop, and the disease will be more aggressive than in people without such mutations. A male child with the mutation may also eventually develop breast cancer, but this happens far less frequently. The risk of cancer goes up steadily with age: about twenty per cent by age forty, forty per cent by age fifty. Very rarely do women under thirty develop the cancer, and the chances of cancer pass the fifty per cent mark only around the age of fifty-five. So throughout human history, a woman would most likely become sick after she had given birth to and raised her children. For modern women, particularly western Jewish professional ones who have children later, the mutation may bring cancer before the child-rearing years are past.

Mathematically, women are just as likely to inherit this breast-and-ovarian mutation from their fathers, but they are not as likely to suspect it they have it unless their mothers have been stricken. Because in most countries this sort of genetic testing is not routine (an exception is Israel, where the mutation is relatively common), women who discover they carry the mutation often come from matrimonial cancer dynasties: mothers, grandmothers, great-grandmothers, and sisters in every generation have had the cancers. These women are terrified of having daughters. Some of these women hate their mothers.

That these mutations were discovered first among Jewish women is probably largely, though not entirely, an accident. Jews are an obvious choice for the study of genetics: they make up compact populations certain to share many genetic traits. So do Icelanders, Scandinavians and a large number of other ethnic groups, but they are not as frequently found near large medical-research centres. It may also be that Jewish medical researchers have chosen to study familiar communities.

My generation, making radical and underinformed decisions, may be lucky to be the guinea pigs—or not. In the last ten years a few thousand mostly Jewish, mostly midlife women, mostly in the US and Israel, have gained the kind of knowledge humans are unfamiliar with having. I have had my fortune told by a genetic counsellor at a hi-tech medical centre in Boston.

My daughter was born nine years after my mother died. I gave her my mother's name: Yolka. She has fashioned it into a story of life. 'You know,' I recently heard her tell a friend of mine. 'Before, I used to be a small baby. Then I was born. Now I have grown and become a girl. Before, I used to be Grandmother Yolka, but I died.'

The calm simplicity of that story pleases me, but I worry now about what I have passed on. My overconfidence about my own hereditary fortune affected my daughter too: when I gave her my mother's name, I was certain she would take only the best. Women who know they have a cancer-gene mutation are, I have discovered, rarely so cavalier. I have talked to young women who would rather adopt a child with an entirely unknown health history, than risk passing the possibility of breast cancer on to a daughter. I have talked to older women who are wracked with guilt over having passed on the mutation. I have talked to a woman who hates her eighty-four-year-old mother for being cancer-free while she and all her sisters, who inherited the mutation, have developed cancer. They focused their anger on the mother's refusal to be tested for the mutation—as though it would have made a difference—and when she finally relented, and tested positive, they rejoiced in the chance to lay blame.

With a disease as unpredictable as cancer, the opportunity to blame an actual person is an unexpected temptation. Often mutations can be traced through generations, based on the history told by death certificates, obituaries, and fears passed on from mother to daughter. I have talked to women who have seen their mothers, grandmothers, aunts, sisters and cousins struggle with cancer and succumb in a pattern that becomes familiar. My own mutation goes back to my mother, who got it from her father (he was killed in the Second World War at the age of twenty-two, but his sister later developed ovarian cancer, pinpointing their branch of the family as the culprit). My grandfather and great-aunt seem to have got the mutation from my great-grandfather, who died of colon cancer in his early sixties (mutation carriers seem to have a slightly increased risk of colorectal cancer as well). Then the trail gets lost, as it often does, since in chains of mutation-carriers generations seldom overlap by much: most of my other great-grandparents lived to see me born, but this one died years before I came along.

The first time I went to a gathering of women who carry the breast-and-ovarian-cancer mutation, I found myself looking hard into their faces, looking for familiar features. Unlike, say, people with HIV or multiple sclerosis, we share more than a similar condition, parallel concerns and identical hopes: we have common blood. The current mainstream scientific thinking is that mutations like ours do not occur spontaneously at different times in different populations. These mutations are sometimes called 'point mutations', to indicate that the sequence of the gene is not scrambled but simply that one allay (the one coding for the 189th protein, in my case) is punched out. These mutations are thought to have what is called a 'founder effect'—that is, to go back to one person. The fact that my particular mutation is found among both Ashkenazi and, albeit less often, Sephardic Jews, means the 'founder' was a very distant ancestor, someone who lived long before the split into Ashkenazim and Sephardim. It is also one more piece of proof that these two groups have a common root.

That is why one can refer to these mutations as 'Jewish' without incurring the wrath of the politically correct, as long as they can make the leap—especially difficult for Americans—to thinking of Jewishness as an ethnicity rather than a religion. That can explain, for example, why a Catholic population in the American southwest that traces its roots to a ship that sailed from Spain in the fifteenth century, has a high incidence of the same mutation that I got from my mother: the sailors were probably Jewish before they became Catholics. The cutting-edge science of the twenty-first century has a way of turning one's thinking about blood, religion and disease positively medieval.

I looked around the room at the women carrying my mutation. They looked nothing like me, but many of them had the thick post-chemo hair, the brittle post-chemo skin and the protruding breast prostheses that reminded me of my mother. The hospital where my mother had her mastectomy and where I now go for my breast MRIs was across the street. But she was not here.

When I learned of my mutation in January 2004, I was thirty-seven, my daughter was two and a half, and her brother—who is adopted—was nearly seven. I had been thinking of having another child. My cumulative risk of breast cancer was roughly fourteen per cent. I was, in the absurd argot of the trade, a 'previvor': not yet diagnosed with cancer but with a high risk of getting it. I went to see a genetic counsellor.

Those who learn that they carry a mutation like mine are immediately admitted to the cancer caste. I found myself carrying a cancer centre's patient card, walking past a wig-and-prosthesis shop on my way to see my doctors, and retracing my mother's steps down the hospital corridors—still hoping that in my version, the same genes will add up to a better life, and a longer one.

The genetic counsellor, her head permanently cocked to one side in a show of sympathy, suggested there was only one way out of the cancer ward. She advised me to cut out my ovaries. She said I might also consider removing my breasts. I was still using them to feed and comfort my daughter then. Breast milk had turned out to be the magic potion of motherhood: it nourished my daughter during her frequent illnesses when she was a baby, and it could fix frustration, anxiety or a stubbed toe once she became a toddler.

I spent weeks reading medical studies and doing frantic arithmetic, careening from one option to another. In the end I leaned towards chest surgery, but I decided to proceed slowly. I weaned my daughter. I managed to convince her that big girls do not drink from the breast. It took a couple of weeks and then she took to holding my breasts, which she still does—before she goes to sleep, when she wakes up, or for comfort when she has hurt herself or feels insulted. Every time I cuddle her, I worry: how can I get rid of them when she needs them? The argument that ought to trump them all—that any trauma is worth it if it means having me around—doesn't convince me. What worries me, gnaws at me to the point where I feel a stabbing pain in my chest—my breast—is the fear of losing the physical connection with my daughter that I never remember having with my mother. It was there as sure as the fact that I bolted awake the moment she died 3,000 miles away, but I never felt it. Touching her did not give me comfort.

There is a black-and-white picture of me at the age of perhaps two months, my mother holding me. My mother, her lips buried in the black down on my head, has that look of being desperately tired and profoundly in love, a look—or, rather, a state—I recognize. This is the last evidence that we had that connection. When I walked into her hospital room at Boston's Brigham and Women's Hospital in August 1990, she pointed with her chin toward the flatness under her gown and said, 'I fed you with that breast.' She sounded like she was saying something one said in such situations. I mumbled something non-committal, which is to say, unfeeling: I felt nothing.

In the two years between my mother's operation and her death, we tried, through short phone calls and more-frequent visits, to make up for whatever it was we had lost. Our progress was uncertain, and we both believed the effort was doomed. Six months before my mother's death, I stayed with my parents for a few weeks. As I was leaving, my mother said she had written a letter to her own mother boasting that we had managed to spend all that time together without fighting. That was our accomplishment; intimacy and affection were beyond reach. When we were saying goodbye, my mother hugged me and whispered, 'Be happy, my girl.' I was giving a talk the next day in the same town, but my mother was too weak to come. I never saw her alive again.

During those two years I developed a habit of thinking of my mother as I got on a plane. After years of little air travel, I started flying a lot soon after my mother was diagnosed—and discovered I had a paralyzing fear of flying. Then I found that when I thought of my mother, imagined her face and voice, the fear abated and a sort of calmness set in: I usually fell asleep just before take-off. The psychobabble in my head said that when I thought of the unexpected calm with which my mother was facing her own death, it made it easier to consider even the possibility of an air crash. I now think the mechanism was simpler: thinking of my mother was enough to calm me because one is never really mortal as long as one has a mother.

When I boarded a small plane in Palm Springs on August 22, 1992, a half-price mourner's ticket across the country in my hand, the old panic grabbed me without warning. I tried to visualize my mother, but the trick did not work. I saw her face, I heard her voice, but the fear only deepened. I no longer had a mother. For perhaps as long as twenty years we had denied each other the affection of a mother and daughter. For ten years I had lived separately. But only then, at the age of twenty-five, boarding a plane to go and bury my mother, did I feel finally untethered and unprotected.

My daughter will go on in the world with feet and eyebrows that are replicas of mine, a stubbornness just like mine, and the habit—my habit—of scrunching up her face when doing something that requires great concentration, such as colouring between the lines. Most importantly, she will carry with her the memory of me, perhaps even the physical sense of me, and maybe that will be enough to make her feel safe even after I am gone. I think about this in the sleepless early mornings, when she presses her hot heels into the small of my back, and I know I am the only thing that protects her from the cold wind of fear and freedom that comes into the room through the open balcony door. Then she taps me on the shoulder and asks me to turn around so she can hold my breasts. □

Can you judge a book by its cover?

The Granta Diary 2005 is for everyone who loves books, with 53 striking book jacket designs in full colour, chosen from a hundred years of publishing history, with important dates for life and literature in the year ahead.

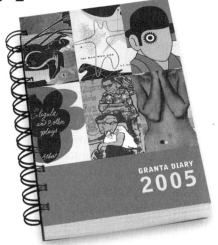

WEEK-TO-VIEW • SPIRAL-BOUND • A5 DESK SIZE • INTERNATIONAL HOLIDAY DATES LITERARY ANNIVERSARIES, FAMOUS FIRST AND LAST LINES AND LOTS MORE INDISPENSABLE LITERARY STUFF

1 86207 668 5 • £9.99 inc. VAT (£8.50 ex-VAT)
Available from all good bookshops or direct from www.granta.com

www.granta.com

GRANTA

THE COLLECTOR

TEXT BY PAUL MALISZEWSKI

PHOTOGRAPHS BY STEVE FEATHERSTONE

Joseph Mitchell in lower Manhattan, c. 1970.

The Collector

On December 19, 1970 the writer Joseph Mitchell crossed the Hudson River from Manhattan to scavenge in the condemned Hoboken Ferryhouse. Its windows were knocked out, the paint was peeling and the tin roof rolled back on itself. Broken glass, old newspapers, rags and trash covered the floors. Mitchell, a reporter for *The New Yorker* whose reputation as one of the city's best chroniclers survived mostly in the memories of a small number of devoted readers, wandered around as his wife Therese, a photographer, took pictures. In one, he tugged on a fence. In another, he stooped to examine a stair rail. He removed an illuminated sign that read NEXT BOAT from a wall, then collected the curved brackets that held it in place, as well as the nuts, bolts, screws and washers. He bagged them all and jotted down the date and some notes about their location.

A month later, Mitchell went back to the Ferryhouse and found two small screws. He put them and a note scrawled on the back of a business card—'Screws (for size), from bench, Hoboken Ferryhouse, January, 1971'—in a plastic bag, closed it with a twist-tie, and went home.

I first learned of Mitchell's collecting in an article about him by Mark Singer in *The New Yorker*. Singer described Mitchell's 'odd treasures—glass bottlenecks, New York hotel spoons, brass hinges' and suggested that all these bits of Mitchell's past 'gave him far more comfort than the present'. I got in touch with Mitchell's daughters, Nora Sanborn and Liz Mitchell, who now keep what their father collected from the streets of New York and the fields of North Carolina. Nora invited me and Steve Featherstone, a photographer and a friend, to her house in New Jersey to have a look.

In Nora's dining room there was a white basin full of forks, some from New York hotels. Glassware, china and silver filled the shelves. I counted eleven drawers full of keyhole covers and pulls. Elsewhere rusty iron signs, some in fragments, were stamped with names from New York's industrial past ('Lackawanna Railroad' and 'Automatic Fire Alarm Co, 416 Broadway'). Loose notes in Mitchell's hand read 'Atlantic Iron Works nameplate (in four pieces—three in a plastic bag, one loose)' and 'LOOK IN THESE GULLIES MORE CLOSELY IN THE FUTURE'. Mitchell's guidebooks—about cemeteries, about apples, about slums—were stuck full of his notes and bookmarks.

Paul Maliszewski

In the basement there was a gas meter we couldn't move and a lithography stone for printing business forms. Nora brought up several large boxes and a plastic Postal Service bin for us to root through. Each was full of the jars, capsules and bags in which her father had saved things: lone nails, spent shotgun shells, a feather. Most had a note inside—often scribbled on the back of an envelope or a scrap of *New Yorker* letterhead—detailing the discovery. Nora said, 'Whatever you see here, there's pretty much twice as much, because my sister and I split it.' Between them, they had shared out fire alarm boxes and tractor seats in the way other siblings split their dead parents' furniture or shares of stock.

Mitchell had especially loved bottles. At Nora's, blue bottles lined the kitchen window, clear glass ones covered a roll-top desk and brown ones crowded a corner. 'He didn't collect those bottles for being pretty,' Nora said. 'He collected them for what they had been... He would be very interested in what was in them. He'd buy one and he'd come home and he had all these bottle books, and he'd sit and look them up, see what it was and look up the history, and then he'd stick it in a trunk.'

Joseph Mitchell was born in 1908 in Fairmont, North Carolina, a small farming town in the swampy south-eastern part of the state. He moved to New York in 1929, just after the stock market crash, and he soon found a job covering the crime beat in Harlem for the *Herald Tribune*. One of his editors advised him that a good reporter should live all over the city, so he moved from apartment to apartment, changing neighbourhoods every month for the first decade he was there. Later, he worked for other New York papers, the *Morning World* and the *World-Telegram*, writing celebrity features about people such as Emma Goldman, Noël Coward and Eleanor Roosevelt.

In 1937, he was hired by *The New Yorker*. His editors there encouraged his wish to write about less-celebrated people, and for the next thirty years he perfected his craft, writing profiles of a bearded lady, the owner and operator of a flea circus, a self-proclaimed naval commodore and a gypsy king; as well as of a couple eking out their existence in a cave in Central Park during the Depression. He described the Mohawk Indians who were building the city's skyscrapers, the old-timers holding down barstools in

Joseph Mitchell at the Hoboken Ferryhouse, New Jersey, December 1970

THERESE MITCHELL

Paul Maliszewski

Greenwich Village taverns, the clam diggers, street preachers, vaudeville performers and fortune-tellers of New York at mid-century. In his most famous article he described Joe Gould, a man whose life's work was to record local conversation, jokes, anecdotes and gossip. Gould estimated he'd written 'approximately nine million two hundred and fifty-five thousand words,' all in notebooks that he'd allegedly squirrelled away in the houses of friends (and no-longer-friends), at favoured restaurants, and in a barn on Long Island. Little of Gould's work ever saw print.

'Joe Gould's Secret' appeared in *The New Yorker* in 1964 and was hailed as Mitchell's best work yet. It was the last story Mitchell published, in *The New Yorker* or anywhere else. According to Roger Angell, for many years an editor at the magazine, Mitchell continued to come in to work 'almost every day for the next thirty-one years and six months'. Others remember hearing him typing. But he never submitted anything new. What Mitchell was working on was the subject of much speculation—a biography of an old friend, or a memoir of his North Carolina youth, or a novel based loosely on his life? Nobody dared ask. A collection of his *New Yorker* articles, *Up in the Old Hotel*, appeared in 1992 and won acclaim and wide sales. In 1996, he died.

Mitchell seemed most drawn to broken bits of New York's past. He collected things from all over New York, but he paid particular attention to lower Manhattan—especially South Street and the Fulton Fish Market, and the neighbourhood that has become known as the Financial District. From the 1960s, many old buildings there were slated for demolition. In some cases they were already piles of rubble, waiting to be carted off in dump trucks. To Mitchell these were prime locations to hunt for architectural details, doorknobs, fragments of floor tile, lengths of wiring ripped out of the walls and cast-iron structural supports—long T-shaped bars which he sought to salvage, with his usual thoroughness, with the nails still attached. Mitchell even retrieved lengths of wrought-iron fence.

In the tobacco fields of North Carolina, to which he often returned, Mitchell collected bits of coal and gravel, as well as Native American arrowheads and pottery shards. He walked the fields around the farm his family had worked for more than two hundred years, looking for whatever the plough or the rains had uncovered. He was often accompanied by his young nephew Jack, who told me that Mitchell's favourite hunting season was spring. 'That's when everything's being planted and ploughed up, or it's right before everything's starting to come up. And there are rains at that time of the year, and things show up pretty good on the ground...'

Mitchell kept much of what he collected in boxes and envelopes folded in thirds and then fastened securely with string. For smaller objects, he used plastic capsules and jam jars from Dean & DeLuca, the gourmet grocery store in New York. He used a Tiffany's jewellery box to store a couple of iron spikes. He put everything neatly away in a closet or a dresser drawer or under a bed.

According to Liz, her parents were always collecting. Therese liked old picture postcards, advertising ephemera and snuffboxes. She and Mitchell both liked brass and silver objects and frequented flea markets. But Mitchell's daughters agree that in the late 1960s, as New York entered a period of rapid and often heedless development, Mitchell's collecting acquired greater urgency. In 1966, the Port Authority of New York and New Jersey began work on the World Trade Center. The construction company closed five streets and demolished 164 buildings, razing a sixteen-acre area. Mitchell and Jack visited the site.

At Nora's house, I found a brick with a long crack running down the side. It was wrapped with string, as if ready for mailing. A pencilled note explained it was from a building formerly located at 316 Washington Street and that Mitchell retrieved it on July 10, 1969. It was the earliest date I saw on any of the New York objects.

Liz sometimes accompanied her father on his collecting trips. To help him remove artefacts from buildings, he bought some tools, which he and his wife referred to as his burglar's tools. 'He was very into string and brown paper and newspapers,' Liz said. 'And, as I remember, he would wrap the tools up. He'd make a little packet. He certainly didn't have a toolbox.' Once, when Mitchell and Liz went into a building, a policeman asked what they were doing. Mitchell said he was making a survey, and the policeman left them to it.

In 1980, after Mitchell's wife Therese died, Nora began to come into the city on Sunday afternoons to go driving with Mitchell. They'd pick a neighbourhood and spend hours driving the streets. 'We'd just

July, 1974, 78 Duane
from_____ in basement

demolition   ↑
            cut head nail
              was here

August, 1974
Brown Marsh Presbyterian Church near
Clarkton, North Carolina
wooden structure built in 1825, replacing one
built in 1787
(it has probably been repaired several times)
A. J. M. II pulled this cut nail from
a rotting weatherboard with his fingers

drive in and out, and in and out,' she remembered. 'He'd say, "Oh, that place is still there." You know, some little brownstone.'

But Mitchell was growing incensed about the rampant destruction of New York in the name of development. 'He was a real purist,' Nora said. 'I never quite got it then, but now I do. Because so much was lost. He was very, very angry about it. Angry about what they put up in place of a lot of those buildings, and how ugly they were, and boring, and soulless, and expensive, and with no integrity. He was always railing about that kind of thing.'

Throughout the city, old buildings were coming down, and New York's eccentrics, Mitchell's subjects and his friends, were being pushed out, displaced by steeper rents and higher prices. 'He grabbed what he could,' Liz said. 'He was rebuilding [the] New York [of] when he first came to the city, all that it was then. He was trying to preserve it, but not in a big, long-winded way. He just delighted in it.'

Mitchell's writing is as full of things as his apartment became, and it remains a vast storehouse of the past. The articles in *The Bottom of the Harbor* feature epic lists of local churches, voluntary organizations and hotels; great rosters of surnames he'd found on the headstones of neglected graveyards; inventories of birds and flowers, weeds and trees; and ships' nets full of 'lobsters, squid, blue crabs, rock crabs, hermit crabs, surf clams, blood clams, bay scallops, sea scallops, cockles, mussels, moon snails, pear conches, sand dollars, starfish, serpent stars, sea anemones, sea squirts, sea mice, sea urchins, and sponges'. Even rats' nests rate catalogues of their contents.

In his story 'Up in the Old Hotel', Mitchell and a friend from the Fish Market explore the disused floors of the Fulton Ferry Hotel. Mitchell describes the stamped-tin ceiling, tongue-and-groove wainscoting and plaster walls the 'colour of putty' and 'crumbled down to the laths in many places'. There are gas fixtures, a round hole where a stovepipe would once have been, a table with a marble top, seltzer bottles 'with corroded spouts, a tin water cooler painted to resemble brown marble, a cracked glass bell of the kind used to cover clocks and stuffed birds, and four sugar bowls whose metal flap lids had been eaten away from their hinges by rust'.

Perhaps Mitchell's collecting was just an integral part of being the

Paul Maliszewski

kind of reporter he was. Taking notes and collecting were part of experiencing the world with real depth, a way to be engaged with it. It was as if Mitchell couldn't see—couldn't really see—anything, unless he was taking notice of it, picking stuff up and jotting things down. One note marked July 1972 reads:

> basement 78 Duane; the el[ectrical] wire belongs on insulator #2; the nails may not be from the oldest part of the bldg—that is, they may be from boards or beams put in during renovations
>
> the insulators come from a [king?] beam going down the center

With enough of these notes, and a sufficient number of recovered artefacts, it wouldn't seem inconceivable to reconstruct the building at 78 Duane Street. James Joyce, whom Mitchell read and reread, wrote of his ambition to make *Ulysses* so detailed that should Dublin disappear, survivors could rebuild it using his novel as a blueprint. Mitchell's writing is a blueprint for a New York which was then disappearing and is now almost lost.

Liz compared her father's collecting to a 'treasure hunt,' then suggested that it was 'a great big puzzle that he was putting together'. But the collection resists analogies. Mitchell gave some things to his daughters as gifts, including a complicated iron apparatus for telling whether a furnace was open and a doorknob from the Plaza Hotel. Liz's wedding reception had been held there, and Mitchell discovered that the knob on the bathroom door was loose. He removed it without her knowing and, when she returned from her wedding trip, presented it to her as a surprise.

I asked Liz why she thought her father had spent so much time collecting things. 'To me, it's kind of like a way of warding off the night or something,' she said. 'He was pretty gloomy, but he had all these interests that kind of kept him from being in despair, I guess.'

□

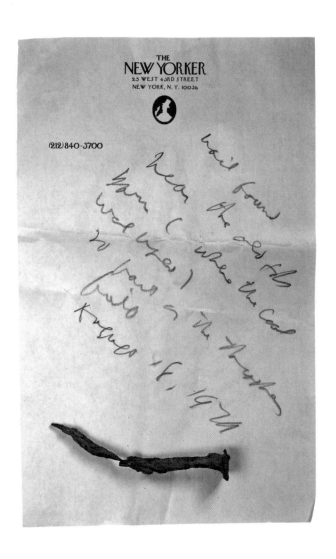

four wire nails (long
and round) are from
bottom piece of frame for
wooden acanthus-leaf box
three cut nails are also
from this frame

THE
NEW YORKER
25 WEST 43RD STREET
NEW YORK, N.Y. 10036

mutilated screw that came out
of the MUNICIPAL BUILDING
doorknob

see if I can find one to
replace it

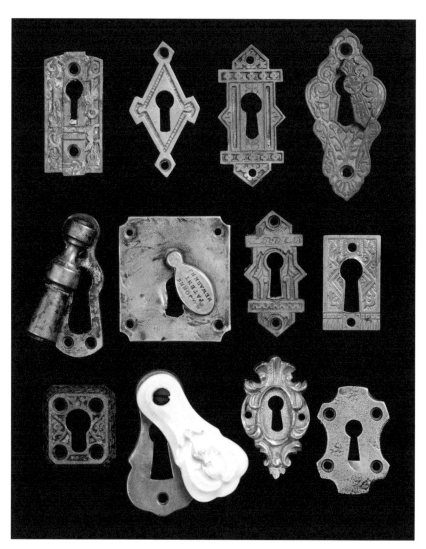

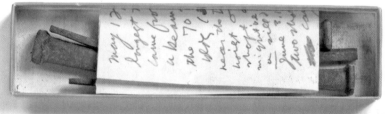

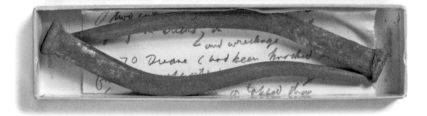

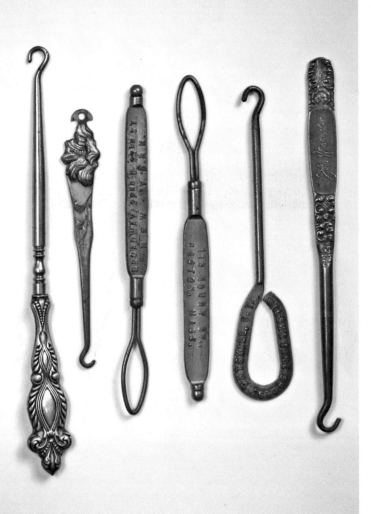

Stone (poss:bly
a hammerstone) picked up
in the Hog Swamp field
(Britt field, my beans).
August, 197?
(picked up my Jack M.)

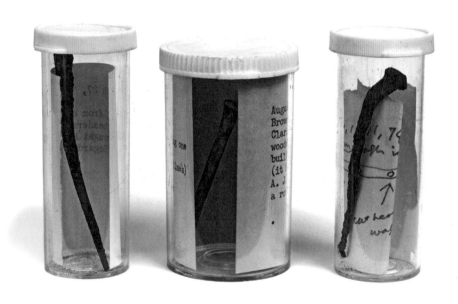

latch, hook,
and broken
screw from
wooden shutter,
second floor
front,
329 Washington
Street (1838)

Friday, September 3, 1971

brass plate from top of motor
on disused hydraulic elevator
installation in mch. basement (and
boiler room) of 16 - 18 Reade St
(I have the foundry plate
from the corner of this bldg nearer
Elk St (there is a narrow alley in between
it and Elk))

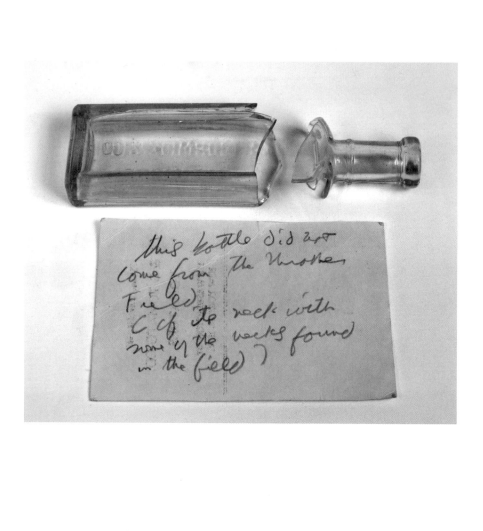

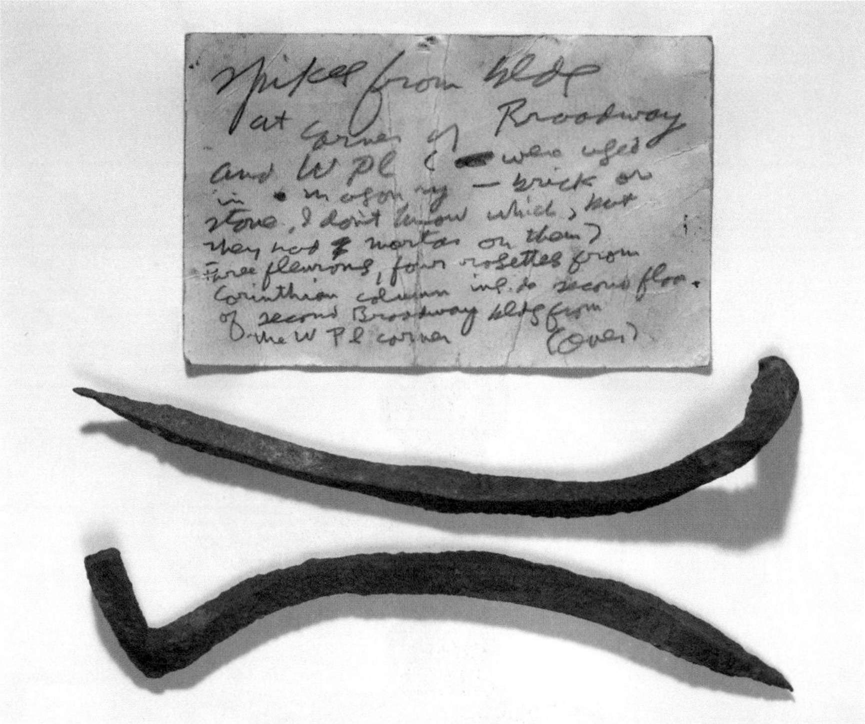

ATLANTIC
IRON WORKS

name plate
(in four pieces — three
in a plastic bag, one loose)

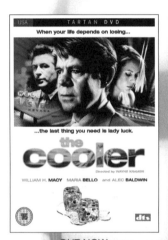

GRANTA

MOTHER OF THE YEAR

Paul Theroux

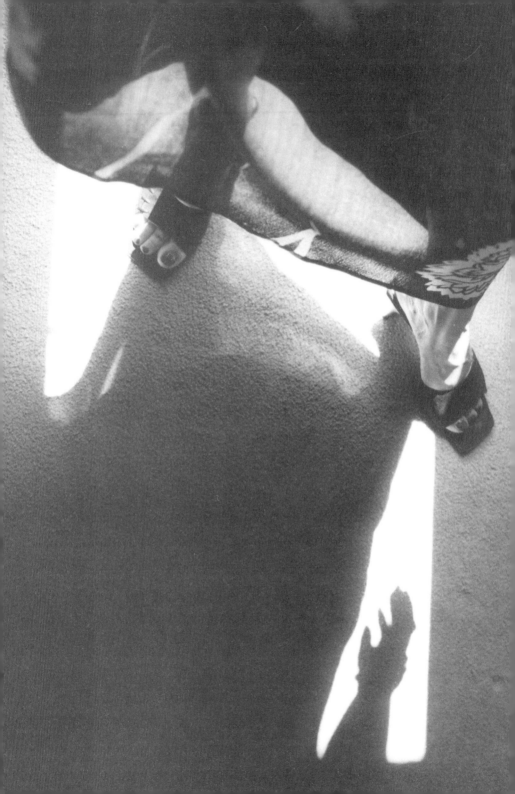

The words 'big family' have the same ring for me as 'savage tribe', and I now know that every big family is savage in its own way.

There were altogether eight of us children, and one of us was dead. Our parents were severe and secretive, and seemed ancient to us, but as long as they were alive, no matter how doddering, we remained their much younger and unformed children. That was how we behaved towards one another, too, childishly, with pettiness and envy. The taunting was endless, and later, all these big stumbling teasers, bulking and bullying, middle-aged pot-bellied kids, mocking each other with fat fingers.

Each of us had the same father—he was solid, though he was often ill. Because of Mother's fickleness, her injustice, her disloyalty, and her unshakeable favouritism, each of us—dealing with our own version of her—had a different mother. Father's illnesses made her impatient and competitive—he was burdened by rotting lungs and arthritic joints and clotted eyes—and at last he was worn out. He said, 'When you're old you never have a good day.' Mother countered that she was ill in retaliatory moans. But Mother was healthy, a robust complainer; she declaimed her ailments with the whining defiance I later came to associate with all hypochondriacs.

Mother's stories and confidences varied, according to which child she was talking to. I should have guessed this early on, because her habit was to see each of us alone, like a wicked tyrant conspiring in a dark fable. She did not entertain us as a group. She encouraged us to visit her separately and hinted that she loved to be surprised with presents. But the phone call was her preferred medium of communication; it allowed for secretness and manipulation. She liked the unexpectedness of a ring, the power of hanging up. In seven phone calls—needy people are chronic phoners—she would tell seven different versions of her day, depending on which of her children she was talking to.

It might be Fred, the eldest, the only child she deferred to and respected. He was a lawyer. She poured out her heart to him and he responded, 'This is what you should do, Ma.' Or it might be Floyd, second oldest, whom she despised and feared, saying, 'He never was right.' He was a university professor and a poet. Or the sisters, Franny and Rose, both of them hoggishly fat and conspiratorial, both of them teachers of small children. Or Hubby, the gloomy one, of whom she said, 'He's so good with his hands.' He was a hospital technician, with a fund of gruesome stories. Or Gilbert, her favourite, a diplomat. 'He's so busy, poor kid, but I'm proud of him.' Or me, known from birth as JP. Mother was circumspect with me, blinking in uncertainty when I visited her and always eager for me to leave. She had wanted me to be a doctor—she had never liked my being a writer and when someone praised a book of mine, she said, 'Oh?' and made a face as though she'd been poked with a stick. Mother spoke to Angela, too, though through the power of prayer, not on the phone; Angela was the dead one.

This infant girl had died at birth, her life snuffed out when she was hours old, yet she had a name ('She was like an angel'), she had a personality and certain lovable quirks and was part of the family. She was often mentioned as the perfect one, whom we should emulate. Angela was more conspicuous and present, much more available for advice and consolation—and even guidance—because of her being a spectre. Such ghostly presences often dominate the daily life of savage tribes. When Mother needed an ironclad excuse or a divine intervention, it came from Angela, who was the most powerful and prescient, warning Mother of disloyal whispers or dangerous portents. Angela not only had a name and a personality, she even had a history. She was mourned every January 8, a day when Mother was paralysed with grief and needed to be visited or phoned, in order to pour out her sorrow and the story of her difficult pregnancy, fifty years ago. Dead Angela was also necessary in helping to plump out the family, like the fictional dead souls in the Gogol novel, making our big family even bigger.

'Big family' does not mean a congenial crowd to me; it suggests disorder, treachery, greed and cruelty, an old-fashioned clan of close relations that is the nearest thing in civilization to a cluster of cannibals. I am generalizing here, using the words 'savages' and 'cannibals' for emphasis and for the colour of melodrama, and I know unfairly. Reading those words you are immediately put in mind of comic, half-naked bone-in-the-nose jungle dwellers, bow-and-arrow people, beating drums and dangerous only to themselves in their recreational violence; and of course hollering and jumping on big feet and showing their teeth. Such people don't exist in the real world. I once lived in the Equatorial regions where these belittled stereotypes are said to live, and I found the folk there to be anything but savage; they were subtle, chivalrous, open-hearted, dignified and generous. It was in suburban America that I encountered savagery in its riskiest form and recognized all the mythical characteristics associated with cannibals in my own big flesh-and-blood family.

My father was the henpecked chief, my mother his tyrant consort of the cannibal tribe that went under the name of a big family. Dissatisfied and frustrated, we were a collection of unruly people struggling for dominance, relentless rivals getting away with murder. We had our own language and customs, our peculiar pieties, grievances and anniversaries, all of them incomprehensible except to the family members themselves. Also, though we were moody, merciless and full of envy, we were always pretending to be the opposite. The solid seamless hypocrisy of religion was an asset: big families are nearly always attached to a fanatic and unforgiving faith. Ours was. You don't think happy or sad, you think of the fury of survival and of damnation and blame.

Such families hardly exist any more in the planning-conscious western world of tiny houses and limited space and rising costs. The birth rate in Europe is recorded in negative numbers, hinting at shrinking populations and small families. This is why the story of any large family is worth telling, because such families have been forgotten. Yet the members of these complex and crazed clans have helped shape the world we know now, probably for the worse.

'Big happy family', people used to say of us, and we smiled, for we believed there was no such thing. Yet happy was how we advertised ourselves, because we had so much to hide. Cynicism is another big family attribute. Some of our desperation must have arisen from the fact that we knew our family was a dinosaur, too big to survive, too clumsy to flourish, too embarrassing to expose to strangers. We were a grotesque phenomenon from another century, a furious and out of date tribe at war with itself, ruled over by a demented queen.

When I read or hear about a mother who dotes on her children, who works her fingers to the bone (Mother's self-regarding catchphrase); who often invites her children to visit her, or who visits them with presents—a kindly-seeming woman, full of solemn, stern advice—I think: What on earth does the sententious old woman want? She can only be wicked and manipulative to be so persistent; and whoever trusts her has got to be a fool. She will eat you alive.

As a child I believed my mother was a saintly and self-sacrificing woman—a little tedious and repetitive, but virtuous and on my side. For a long time I went on believing it. Of course, she fostered this fiction, she worked at shaping it, she did not tolerate dissent. And I was also influenced by her public image, for she was something of a local celebrity: a former schoolteacher respected by her students, active in church affairs, shrewd about money, insightful in matters of the heart, a pious busybody beloved by everyone except us, who only feared her unreasonable demands. To the world at large my mother was a resourceful and hardworking woman who had raised seven children (and nurtured the memory of the eighth) and put them through college, the matriarch of a big happy family. She identified with wise and long-suffering Mother figures in the news, especially the annual Mother of the Year, whom she never saw as a role model but always as a rival. She even compared herself with the mothers depicted in the comics—'Mary Worth' was one—and also the sensible grey-bunned soul in the early TV series, *I Remember Mama*. But she also prayed hard to the Virgin Mary, and in all her piety there was the presumption that she and the Mother of God had much in common as nurturers and advice-givers.

I marvel at my innocence, for Mother was the nearest thing to a witch I have ever known. She seldom told the truth—no, she never told the truth. To be fair, I don't think she knew what the truth was. Even Wittgenstein said, 'Why tell the truth when it is to your advantage to lie.' In her perversity, whatever she wanted you to believe that day was the truth. She would do anything to get your attention—be angry, upset, abusive, even gentle in a foxy way. Sick, too: she could make herself noticeably ill so that we would listen to her. She might also offer us presents, but they were the sorts of simple tokens that simple folk exchanged in the jungle.

She never gave us money, for to do that would reveal to us that she had some, and her mantra was that she had none. Money did not exist in our family as a fact, only as an abstraction, something whispered about, so hard won it was almost unattainable. I might see a few dollars in a wallet or some coins in a purse but I never saw more than that. A wad of money, a thick roll of bills, was absurd fantasy. And because it was unseen, magic was attached to money, but a wicked magic, a kind of curse. We did not think we deserved to have money, and if by chance we got some we could not spend it, because spending was wasteful. Money in your pocket tripped you up, made you fail; you were better off without it.

Money was a thing of darkness; always put away. Money was something that was saved—stacked up, hoarded, stashed for a rainy day, but always small amounts scraped into a pile, like Father winding knotted lengths of string into a ball; but why? We didn't ask.

Money was whispered about because it was tainted. Other people had it—we did not; we would never have it. We had no idea where money came from. We did not know anyone who had it. The ways in which other people got money were a mystery to us.

Money did not grow on trees. Money was the root of all evil. Money was filthy lucre. A fool and his money were soon parted. Most people had more money than brains. They spent money like a drunken sailor. They knew the price of everything and the value of nothing.

We were so in awe of the rich that we were forbidden to use the word. Instead of 'They're rich,' we had to say, 'They're comfortably off.' Rich families were like members of another species, but a dangerous one that needed to be propitiated with our being submissive. We saw them as conquering tribes; the world belonged to them. We were moneyless and so powerless.

At first, when Mother claimed to have no money, we took her at her word, and pitied her a little. We got part-time jobs and gave her half our weekly pay. 'This will go towards the electric bill,' Mother would say, 'This will help pay for your food.' That was her way of saying it would never be enough. We went on owing her, paying off a debt that had no end.

Later, from vague hints and chance remarks, we suspected that Mother had some money, somewhere. Perhaps her bleak insistence that she was poor was the giveaway. 'I'm wearing a dead woman's dress,' she once said, to emphasize her poverty—a morbid hand-me-down, with the stink of death still on it. That shocked us. If she paid for something for us, she made such a fuss we felt so bad we never asked again. She had no chequebook; she never used credit. She paid in cash, though she always concealed these transactions from us to maintain the fiction that she had no money. Paying for something

in cash was probably the most solemn of her secret ceremonies.
Father had nothing to do with money. He handed over his pay
to Mother at the end of the week. He never mentioned money.
Mother set us against one another, played favourites, mocked one
to another, and when hectoring didn't work she belittled us. I found
a ghastly joy in this mockery. I would visit and without any cue from
me she would talk about Fred's wife, who had just called to wish her
well. What a slattern she was, very messy, never cooked a proper meal,
always kept Fred waiting—and Fred always came home from work
to a bad meal and an unappreciative wife. Or she would tell a long
satirical story of Fred's wedding day, what a charade it had been, how
his in-laws had undermined him. Or Floyd had just sent her a nasty
letter, much too abusive for her to show it to me. 'Do I deserve that?'
Mother rolled her eyes when Hubby's name was mentioned—Hubby
was fat and slow and was always making conspicuous and needless
improvements to his house, 'his castle', Mother said, and pulled a face.
Rose was not only the victim of her two children but of her husband,
as well, a fanatical baseball fan. 'When the Red Sox lose he's
impossible.' Gilbert was her favourite, 'but he never visits'. Franny she
jeered at for being over-affectionate and careless with money and a soft
touch—a sucker: she was a fool for catering to her ungrateful children.
    Mother resented all the spouses and disliked her grandchildren.
She was particularly hard on Janine, Franny's eldest—memories of
tantrums, howling fits, stubbornness, scenes. 'Remember Janine
kicked the windshield out of the car by bracing herself on the front
seat?' One of the other daughters took ballet lessons. 'Grace is a
reindeer,' Franny said. 'In *The Nutcracker*.' But even these dancing
lessons were regarded by Mother as a foolish expense and she found
humour in 'Grace is a reindeer.' Franny's husband was a security
guard. He was a big frightened man with fat pale cheeks and a belly
swollen with doughnuts, so Mother said. He had a habit of locking
himself in the bathroom for hours on end. He patrolled a local
shopping mall and carried a cellphone in a holster as though it was
a pistol. Mother mocked him for his belly, his fear, his ulcers, his
sweet tooth, his lack of ambition. He did not deserve Franny.
    In the canniest way, she asked me what I had heard; pretended
not to know anything so as to compare my version of a story with
the one she had already been told, and was hungry for the smallest

detail of frailty or foolishness. Her eyes glittered with pleasure at a choice piece of gossip, and hearing something truly wicked she could not prevent herself from laughing out loud.

My reward for visiting her was that she confided these things. Sometimes the betrayals took my breath away. Hubby had just visited for lunch. He had asked for seconds. 'He's put on so much weight. His clothes are almost bursting. If he keeps on like this he's going to explode.' Or it was Fred's ex-wife, who had brought her a lamp. 'She must have found it in a thrift shop. There was a crack in the base. I think she wants to electrocute me.' Or Rose's overbearing husband: 'I understand they're in family counselling. Do you think he still drinks?' She jeered at her own children for their pretensions, and at their spouses for incompetence or greed. Her cruellest remarks were aimed at members of her family, Angela excepted.

None of this seemed particularly unfair to me; all of it was the cruel comedy of a normal visit or phone call. And somehow I felt uplifted, for I was always flattered to think that she was singling me out to disclose these truths to me. I never defended any of these people—in fact, I added more gossip to it; I piled it on. It was as though in gossiping to me and running the other children down Mother understood my resentments, my rivalry, all my hurts. They deserved it.

The disclosures about the others made me happy in many petty ways; I felt wanted, I felt secure, hearing Mother's secrets. It did not ever occur to me that, with another member of the family, she would ever speak in this reckless way about me—my spending, my size, my children, my ex-wives.

All that is horrible, but here is something I regard as more shameful still. This woman was quite old before I was able to admit to myself who she really was.

But nothing was obvious to me about my family, or the world around it, until Father died.

We were all summoned from our homes and told Father was ill—seven phone calls as well as a prayer to Angela. Mother called each of us in turn. She said something different to each of us. 'I think you should be here,' she told me. To Fred: 'As the eldest it's up to you to take charge.' To Floyd: 'Dad's ill. I think he'd like you to be there.' To Franny, 'I don't think I can manage without you.'

To Rose: 'Franny will need your help.' To Hubby: 'We'll need you
to do the driving.' To Gilbert: 'Your Father's been so difficult lately.
I've felt like hitting him.'

We did not know until it was too late that we had been asked to
gather in order to witness him die.

The sterility of the hospital was like a preparation for his going—
the cold place seemed like an appropriate antechamber to a tomb.
Though the antiseptic smell made me think only of ill health, nothing
was familiar in this unornamented place, nothing at all that I could
associate with Father, who was untidy, and frugal, and like many
frugal people not a minimalist but a pack rat. Father was a hoarder
and piler of junk, a collector of oddments, a rifler of dumpsters. His
garage had the stacked shelves you see in a Chinese shop, and the
same dense and toppling asymmetry too. He would take two barrels
of trash to the landfill and return with three barrels of items he had
rescued—old pots, broken tools, jelly jars, kindling wood, coils of
old rope. 'That'll come in handy some day,' he would say.

The hospital room was neat and bare, except for the man in the
bed, who lay like wreckage under the complex apparatus monitoring
his heart and lungs. Mother remained in the corridor, signalling for
each of us to slip in and greet Father. We had not been together this
way for years, and towards evening, we grouped around his bed to
pray for him, looking less like children than like superstitious jungle
dwellers muttering to the gods, the first intimation I had after so
many years that we were at heart nothing but savages.

Father struggled to speak, then gasped on his ventilator, 'What a
lovely reunion.' Barely had we recovered from the shock of seeing
him reduced in this way when Mother ordered us all into the hospital
corridor. Standing there, looking strong, she took charge and said,
'We think it's best to take him off his ventilator. He's so
uncomfortable.' Taking him off the ventilator meant: Let him die. I
started to object, but she interrupted. 'The doctor says he doesn't
have long.' She was glassy-eyed and seemed determined, not herself
but a cast-iron version of herself, so nerved for the occasion and
standing so straight she seemed energized, even a bit crazed, as
though defying any of us to oppose her. She was eighty years old,
though she was so sure of herself you would have taken her for a
lot less. I did not know her. She was a stranger, a substitute—fierce,

deaf to advice, domineering, wilful, sure of herself. She was not the tremulous old woman who had suffered through Father's illness; she was someone else entirely, a woman I scarcely recognized.

I said, lamely, 'Where there's life there's hope'—and thought, 'uncomfortable' is better than 'dead'.

'Don't you see this is for the best?' she said, in a peevish tone that implied I was being unreasonable. It was the tone she used when she said, 'The TV is on the fritz. Junk it.'

Her implication was that I was being weak and obstructive. He ought to be allowed to die, she was saying, in a merciful way; while I was urging her to let him live, something she regarded as cruel, inhumane and insensitive. And I was misinformed.

'What's the point of letting him suffer?'

'Why don't we all go out for a meal?' Gilbert said.

Franny and Rose stood on either side of Mother, less like daughters than like newly appointed ladies-in-waiting. They were bent over in grief. They were enormous, humpbacked with fat, panting and draped in sweat-stained clothes.

'I think I'll stay with Dad,' I said.

'We should keep together,' Mother said.

'We could all stay with Dad.'

She said, 'Let's just leave him in peace,' again, in that tone that implied I was being uncooperative and cruel.

'Let's do what Ma says,' Franny said.

'It's not asking too much,' Rose added.

Mother just smiled her challenging smile.

'I don't know.'

Fred said, 'You should do what you think is right.'

Floyd said, 'I don't get this at all. This is like climbing Everest with Sherpas, and traversing the edge of the crevasse, all roped together. Dad slips and he's dangling on a rope way down there, and we don't know whether to cut him loose and leave him or drag him down the mountain. And there's a blizzard. And we can't hear what he's saying.'

Hubby said, 'That's it, make a big drama.'

'Oh, right, sorry, it's not dramatic. It's only Dad dying. I forgot, Hubby.'

'Asshole,' Hubby said.

'I'd like to kick you through that wall,' Floyd said.

Paul Theroux

Franny said, 'Let's not fight.'

'You're all upsetting Ma,' Rose said.

'God knows I do my best,' Mother said, not in her usual self-pitying whine but defiantly.

We went to a nearby restaurant. Fred whipped off his eyeglasses, surveyed the menu and, as the eldest of us, and being Fred, ordered the set meal for everyone. We sat like mourners, though Father was four blocks away, still alive. I looked at the faces around the table, Mother at the head of it, between Gilbert and Fred, the girls Franny and Rose close by, all of them watching Mother in a way I can only describe as loyal and submissive, squinnying at the rest of us, while Hubby and Floyd sat with their heads down, looking torn.

'It's going to be all right,' Franny said.

'This is for the best,' Rose said.

I had been listening to such clichés my whole life, but I think it was there in the restaurant, knowing how Father was dying and we were here eating with Mother, that I realized how clichés always reveal the deepest cynicism.

Franny and Rose heaved themselves towards Mother and said, 'Have some bread, Ma.'

'Dad would have wanted it this way,' Mother said. 'All of us together.'

I quietly excused myself, an easy thing to do, everyone at the table assuming I was going to the men's room. I had often done that as a small boy in Sunday school. 'Please, Father.' And the priest in the middle of a pep talk would wave me on my way; and I would go home.

I went back to the hospital and found Father alone. The nurse told me that he had been taken off his ventilator and, in place of the saline IV, was on a morphine drip. The fearful look in his eyes appalled me. He was like a terrified captive being dragged away to an unknown place against his will—which was exactly what was happening. I held his hand; it was warm and had the softness of someone very ill. The morphine dulled the pain but it also weakened him and loosened his grip on life—I could feel resignation in the slackness of his fingers.

The gauges beside his bed showed his heart rate in a jumping light, the pattern on the screen like that of a depth sounder in a boat tracing the troughs in an irregular ocean floor. The lights and beeps all seemed to me indications of his life, but the pace of them revealed his diminishing strength.

And there was his breathing. What had begun as slow exhalation became laborious and harsh, as though he was not propped up (which he was) but flat on his back, with a demon kneeling on his chest. His breathing gave him no relief, but was like a punishment, seeming to provide no air at all. He fought to inhale but the air stayed in his mouth, did not fill his lungs, and so he went on gasping, getting nowhere, his staring eyes filled with tears. He was wordless with fear.

The nurse stepped in and leaned towards the monitors.

'Is he feeling any pain?' I asked.

'I can increase the morphine,' she said, and I took this to mean yes, he was having a bad time.

'He seems to be struggling.'

'Agonal breathing.'

She said it casually yet it seemed to me an awful expression and much more horrible for being exact.

Father laboured to stay alive but I could see from the lazier lines on one monitor that his strength was ebbing. Still I held his hand. I had no sense of time passing, but at one point his breathing became shallow, and all the needles and indicators faltered and fell. Father's jaw dropped, his mouth fell open. I clutched his hand and pressed it to my face. I kissed his stubbly cheek.

Take me with you, I thought.

The nurse returned soon after. She quickly summed up what had happened.

'Are you all right?' she asked.

'No,' I said.

I walked back to the restaurant, and found that all of them had gone. Of course, four hours had passed. I called Mother.

She said, 'Where have you been? You left the restaurant without telling anyone. You didn't even touch your meal. Fred and the girls ate your fried clams. Everyone's here now. We're talking about Dad, telling stories. So many wonderful memories. Gilbert was just about to call the hospital to see how things are going.'

'He's gone,' I said.

Paul Theroux

The crowded wake at the funeral home in Osterville was a muddle—tragedy and farce combined; all the distant relations meeting after a long time and making jokes in the form of greetings, remarking on how fat or how thin or how bald we had become. And the pieties about Father. Then tears. Then they just hung around and leafed through the albums of snapshots that cousins had brought—children's marriages, grandchildren, vacations, pets and gardens, even pictures of prize possessions, cars and houses, the sort of pictures that boastful and proud savages would haul out at a feast, if savages had cameras.

Mother sat near the casket, enthroned as it were, receiving people who paid their respects—and they too seemed like emissaries from other tribes, the big families who were our relations, several of them even bigger than ours. The look on Mother's face I recognized from the hospital: exalted, even somewhat crazed, with a snake's glittering stare. She sat upright, weirdly energized by the whole business.

More tribal rituals: the funeral mass at the church, the platitudes, the handling of the shiny coffin, the sprinkling of holy water on its lid, the processions and prayers. I kept thinking of naked people in New Guinea performing similar rites: preparing the corpse of an elder and calling upon the gods to protect him and to hurry his soul into the next world. Mother was the sole surviving dignitary, bestowing a kiss on the polished lid of the coffin and walking past the banks of flowers with a slight and smiling hauteur.

We drove to the cemetery in a long line of cars behind the hearse. Mother was in the back seat of the lead car between Franny and Rose, Fred at the wheel, Gilbert next to him. Hubby and his family in the next one; Floyd and I, the divorced sons, behind them.

I asked Floyd about the meal I had missed at the restaurant, when I had snuck out to be with Father.

'I didn't stay,' he said. 'I went for a walk. So did Hubby, but in a different direction. It was just Ma and the others, I guess.'

'I think Ma was pissed off that I didn't stay. Like it was a test of loyalty.'

Floyd wasn't listening. He said, 'This is uncanny,' and turned the radio up:

'Bye-bye, Miss American Pie,/Drove my Chevy to the levee...'

'Remember Grandma's funeral?' Floyd said, and he laughed and shook his head.

One of the footnotes to our family history was that in the procession to Grandma's funeral our cousin Louie, a goofball, had the radio on, and that same song, 'American Pie', was playing, while he sang along with it, drumming on the steering wheel with his grease-monkey's fingers, following Grandma's hearse. None of us ever remarked on it as an insult to the dead woman, only as an extemporized piece of hilarity.

At the cemetery we plodded past gravestones to the hole of the freshly dug grave of Father. The mourners consisted of a procession of mostly members of our own family—spouses, ex-spouses, children, grandchildren, even some great-grandchildren. The rest were near-relations. Hardly any were friends, for my parents were at the age when most of their friends were dead or too ill to show up.

Perhaps this is the place to stress that a big family does not welcome friends, and has no room for strangers; is uncomfortable when they penetrate the privacy of the family and become witnesses and listeners, privy to outbursts and secrets. Even outsiders who are frank admirers are kept at a distance—especially them, for there is so much that must be withheld from them in order to keep their admiration intact. In much the same way, a savage tribe is not just suspicious of strangers but overtly hostile.

As Mother emphasized in her gossip, spouses were outsiders and all of them were mocked, always behind their backs. It could be awkward when one of them caused trouble, but it was worse when they tried to be generous—offered presents, cooked a meal, paid for something. 'Imagine, paying good money for this!' The present was laughable, the meal was a joke, and if they could so easily afford to pay for something, where was the sacrifice? But a dark angry spouse might inspire a measure of respect, if the person was strong, and especially so if the person was a crazy threat, because fear was all that mattered to us. At best, spouses were tolerated, but none of them was liked.

At the time of Father's funeral, neither Floyd nor I was married, and our ex-spouses and children were not present. I wasn't innocent any more. I tried to imagine what my family whispered about each of my two wives, but I knew I would never succeed in capturing the malice; I would underestimate it, and no one would tell me to my face. I knew what hideous things we said about the other spouses, the other children, nephews and nieces. I was relieved to be at the funeral alone, my ex-wives and two children elsewhere. In each case, after we split up, they went far away from me and my big family. Perhaps they always suspected that they were unwelcome, and maybe they also knew how they had been satirized.

The priest stood in the wind, his cloak blowing as he spoke. What he said seemed more like a formula of recited lines than sincere prayers. They were hackneyed and over-rehearsed and it was hard to take him seriously—'Dust to dust, ashes to ashes'—we had all heard them before, and now it was Father's turn. Much of what the priest said was drowned out by the traffic speeding along the road that ran past the cemetery wall.

'...Father, Son and Holy Ghost,' the priest was saying.

'I took the next plane from the coast,' Floyd intoned, wagging his head. Then he said, 'Remember, Grandma used to dig for salad here?'

Mother's mother was a frugal Italian, from another big disorderly family. She dug for dandelions as though they were a great delicacy that only ignorant people would spurn. A cemetery was a good place to dig them because of the wall and the gates that kept dogs out.

Floyd was reminiscing, but he could easily have been trying to make me laugh. Getting someone to laugh at a funeral was one of the skills we had acquired as altar boys. Even Father's funeral was not so solemn an event we wouldn't try to raise a laugh somehow. That wasn't a reflection on our love for Father. Our excuse was, 'He'd have found that funny!'

Our heads were down, we were praying or pretending to. Floyd was humming and murmuring, *This'll be the day that I die*—yes, he was trying to get me to laugh by reminding me of 'American Pie'. I glanced sideways and saw that something else had happened to Mother's face. She wore an expression I had never seen before. Her pious posture, head bowed, shoulders rounded, was that of a mourner, yet her face startled me. The look of hauteur was gone, so were the glittering snake eyes. Hers was a look of relief, of weird jubilation, almost rapture, like someone who has survived an ordeal—weary yet triumphant, full of life and strength.

Father's coffin was not lowered. It remained covered with a velvet cloth. Dropping it into the hole while we watched was probably considered too dramatic and depressing—indelicate, anyway.

A last prayer by the priest, whom I noticed kept mispronouncing Father's name—did this invalidate the prayer?—and we filed back to our cars.

Most accounts of family funerals end here—are in fact an ending. But filing out and leaving Father behind was a beginning, and it began right away, before we left the cemetery.

Mother had been walking slowly towards the parking lot between Franny and Rose, looking small and propped up by her two big daughters, whose fat faces, exaggeratedly solemn, shook with each step.

'Take your time, Ma,' they were saying.

'I got such a lot of guidance this morning talking to Angela. "Be strong, Ma," she said. You know how she is.'

Seeing me about to join the procession, Mother turned and broke away from the girls, and looked herself again, fairly large and confident. She approached me, she squeezed my hands hard.

'I want you to get married. Find someone nice. I want you to do it for me. Will you do that?'

She had that same crazed look in her eyes as when in the hospital corridor she had demanded that Father be taken off the ventilator and said, 'We think it's for the best.'

I didn't know what to say. She had power. The death of her husband—of Father—had transformed her. The king was dead and she, as queen, was absolute monarch of the whole realm. She was eighty years old but in every sense a new life was beginning for her. It would be a long one, too, and eventful enough to fill a book.

'Maybe we should have a little get-together,' Hubby said.

We were standing in the parking lot of the cemetery. Spouses and children stayed a little way off, with the wincing looks of wary people expecting to be abused.

'Dad would have wanted it—something like a family dinner, like the other night,' Hubby said.

'I don't think he would have wanted that,' Rose said. 'He hated restaurants. He always said they were a waste of money.'

'You had your chance and you blew it,' Franny said. 'You walked out of the restaurant the other night. So did Floyd. So did JP. So what's the point?'

Paul Theroux

'It's up to Ma,' Fred said.

We looked at her; for an instant she didn't look strong any more. She made a theatrical gesture, touching her gloved hand to her forehead, and said, 'I've got a splitting headache.'

Franny and Rose rushed to assist her, Gilbert carried her purse, Fred fussed.

The rest of us went our separate ways. In the car, Floyd said, 'Fred's such an asshole. "It's up to Ma." What about his wife? Did you ever see anyone so ugly?'

I called Mother that night, but she did not answer the phone, Franny did.

'She's tired,' Franny said. 'Rose and I are staying here a few more days to look after her. She's had an awful shock. Her nerves are shot.'

But it seemed to me that she had had no shock at all, just a great reward, of health and strength, a renewed vigour, and confidence. She had been proud at the wake, queenly at the cemetery, surrounded by her big family. Her look of power had filled me with apprehension.

I called her the next day and she said she was feeling better, with Franny and Rose staying with her for a few days. Their presence seemed odd, for both of them had jobs that they were obviously neglecting.

Some days later, when she was alone, she called me back: 'I'm sending you a little something. There was money left over from Dad's funeral expenses.'

Mother paid a neighbour to clean out Father's shed—where the tools had been. The garage, too. All of Father's accumulated possessions were junked. The paint cans, the jars of nails, the rope, the wire, the rusty screwdrivers. The yellowed newspaper clippings went. They had been nailed to the wall and some of them were very old: one said WAR IS OVER, another said PEACE AT LAST, the Boston papers from 1945. Some were newspaper pictures of us. Floyd shooting a basket in a high-school gym. Fred bundled up in a hockey uniform, his stick poised and pretending to slap a puck. Me holding a trophy from the Science Fair. Hubby in a group of serious-faced Boy Scouts, en route to a jamboree. Clipped-out mentions of events, such as band concerts and ball games. Others were snapshots. Of Franny and her terrified prom date. Of Franny when she was a nun,

210

draped in her penguin outfit, looking even fatter in her piety. Of Rose, an enormous child in a white dress, hands folded: First Communion. Of Gilbert smiling across the bridge of his violin. Several were attempts at group family photos, but they were amateurish and awkward—there were too many of us, the camera was cheap, we looked a discontented mob.

Father's wood stove was ripped out of the living room. He had kept it burning until the night he was taken to the hospital. No one wanted the old stove. It was so full of ashes when it was moved that they spilled out and the grey dust powdering the floor was a grotesque reminder of him.

'He never did clean it out thoroughly,' Mother said.

I went back to the cemetery about a month later. Father's grave looked new and colourless. I planted some geraniums in front of it, and a small pointed juniper on either side. I told Mother this.

She smiled in pity, as she always did when I made a mistake. She said, 'He's not there, you know.'

She sent me a cheque for $500. I did not need it, and yet I did not know what to do with it, for the dark secret of receiving money from Mother so confused me I kept it to myself.

Franny and Rose were bigger and busier than ever. On their way to Mother's, they stopped off to see me sometimes, bringing me candy and doughnuts, the sort of things they imagined that everyone ate.

'We visit Ma every Sunday,' Franny said one day. Rose just smiled. They were enormous, settled into the cushions of my furniture. The chairs spoke to me; the upholstery groaned, the frames grunted. I was fascinated by the way these pieces seemed so unsuitable, offering so little support, announcing danger. 'We know how busy you are. You don't have to come if you don't want.'

Soon after that, each of them bought a new car.

That year for Mother was the beginning of everything. She had another fifteen vigorous years to live. 'My golden years,' she said, sounding more than ever like a queen. □

A HACKER
MANIFESTO

McKENZIE WARK

Drawing in equal measure on Guy Debord and Gilles Deleuze, McKenzie Wark offers a systematic restatement of Marxist thought for the age of cyberspace and globalization. In the widespread revolt against commodified information, he sees a utopian promise, beyond the property form, and a new progressive class, the hacker class, who voice a shared interest in a new information commons. New in cloth

66 Ours is once again an age of manifestos. Wark's book challenges the new regime of property relations with all the epigrammatic vitality, conceptual innovation, and revolutionary enthusiasm of the great manifestos."
—Michael Hardt, co-author of EMPIRE

McKenzie Wark is Professor of Cultural and Media Studies at Lang College, New School University. He is the author of several books, most recently "Dispositions."

WWW.HUP.HARVARD.EDU HARVARD UNIVERSITY PRESS

GRANTA

NOTES FROM
THE LAND OF NOD
Jim Lewis

These are the ranks of the obsessive, the dissatisfied, the distorted, the strange: drug addicts, fetishists, compulsive cleaners, collectors of cats or snow globes or Caravaggios. Maybe everyone has something like this, large or small, pathological or merely unusual: something that serves, in the pattern of its acquisition or loss, as the measure of how well we're doing. Money, lovers, calories, applause, miles run, roses grown, volumes of Trollope read and reshelved: something to think about, so we don't have to think about anything else. I have mine: I think about sleep.

I think about sleep all the time—more often than I think about love or work, more often than I think about money or death. I'm a connoisseur of sleep, it's my only area of expertise. I think about it the way a river-boat captain thinks about a river; I know all its swells and shallows, where it forks, where it rushes, where the bottom is high.

I covet sleep. I collect it, husband it, save and spend it, count it, sort it, weigh it, and count it again. I can't tell you how much I earned last year, or how many words I wrote, but I know how many hours I spent in bed and how well I slumbered. I have measured out my life with coffee and sleeping pills. I feel guilty if I've slept too much, and when I've slept too little I can't wait to make up the difference. I live my days by how much I've slept the night before, by when I'll nap, by the quality of my exhaustion or alertness.

I am an insomniac. According to one study, there are forty million Americans like me. According to another there are sixty million. Sixty million! Eighty million! Why not more? Why not all of us? No one would know; there's no fellowship here. You can drink in a bar and sober up in the basement of a church, but everyone sleeps (or lies awake) in solitude. To paraphrase Conrad: we dream as we die—alone.

What follows, then, are my confessions, my notes on the art of sleeping, my letters from the land of Nod.

Cusp

Between waking and sleep there lies a no-man's-land, a valley of ashes divided by a river of silvery dreams; short, vivid, anarchic. Travelling here is my favourite thing to do—when consciousness slowly dissolves, and then tips, allowing all of its facts and concerns to come tumbling down, while sweet ghosts whisper nonsense in your ear before passing you back into consciousness. The neighbours lent you their couch, and you lost it, somehow. A friend is feeling your leg and pronouncing it fit for climbing: climbing? You're in the Andes, but you've lost that couch, you can go back if you want, if you can convince them to wait, but they won't wait.

Then it's over. It wasn't a dream, not at this length, with this degree of disconnectedness. It's more like an engine coughing out the last turns of its rotors before dying; or like bits of straw clinging to clothes; or like children hanging wistfully on to an amusement park ride, even though it's stopped turning.

Nod

After killing his brother, Cain complains to God, 'My punishment is greater than I can bear… I shall be a fugitive and a vagabond in the earth; and it shall come to pass, that every one that findeth me shall slay me.' In response, God 'set a mark upon Cain, lest any finding him should kill him'. Well, the Lord does love a paradox: with one gesture he has both punished Cain (identifying him as a transgressor—as, quite literally, a marked man) and protected him (the mark renders him untouchable). Imagine Cain's profound unease, his confusion and guilt. The Bible says that he 'went out from the presence of the Lord, and dwelt in the land of Nod, on the east of Eden'.

In Hebrew, the word *nod* means 'wandering', which is apt to the occasion, and while Jonathan Swift was the first to use 'land of Nod' to mean sleep in the simplest sense, to me it means something more difficult than that: a place of both exile and sanctuary, where I lie awake and wonder what I've done wrong, or sleep as if I were courting oblivion, a fugitive and a vagabond, exactly.

Bedding

I don't understand why we don't spend more money and pay greater care to the place where we spend at least a third of our lives—more time than we spend in an office chair or on a couch or in a car. Only the grave will hold us longer, and who knows what that will be like?

Arranging for sleep is a craft as central to life as cooking. You should know thread count and mattress firmness ratings the way you know when the lamb is done, or how much garlic is too much. For myself, I sleep with the shades drawn; it makes me uneasy to lie down and close my eyes in a room with exposed windows. I feel vulnerable, no matter how dark the night is. I sleep better, and more fully, not just on good sheets but on freshly washed ones, and with some weight on me, so I use a blanket even in a Texas summer, when only very expensive and wasteful air conditioning keeps it from suffocating me. A firm mattress, two firm pillows, a bottle of water on the night table, a book before lights out.

It's possible for a bed to be too good. I once stayed in a hotel room in London where the bed seemed to me the instantiation of an ideal which I had hardly, until that moment, even dared imagine. It was very wide—almost square, actually—and very soft, and the sheets were snowy and cottony and absolutely clean; there were half a dozen pillows of various degrees of firmness, and more in the closet to choose from. I'd arrived there on an overnight flight from central Africa, where I'd spent two weeks sleeping on a narrow cot that sagged so severely my coccyx scraped the floor, and I looked upon this hotel room as a miracle. I expected to sleep deeply there, and I did. But it was a disappointing and sterile sleep, and I awoke rested but unsatisfied, because the experience of sleeping in that bed had no flavour.

Disorders

The disorders of sleep are legion, and they multiply and live off each other. Nightmares and terrors, sleepwalking, bed-wetting, night-sweats, narcolepsy, apnoea, hypopnoea, snoring, periodic limb movements, insomnia, shouting, a sourness in your sleep, the dankness of bad and incomplete dreams. I've been sleeping with my hands twisted under my pillow, bent back on my wrists, my fingers gnarled; the pain of it wakes me in the middle of the night. I don't know why I'm doing it or how to make it stop; even when I lie down for a nap, I find myself jamming my fingers against the cushions.

What's galling is that sleep is supposed to be so natural, so easy—as easy as eating or sex, to name two other activities based on appetite—which risks perversion or failure for those who've somehow lost out on the opportunity to exercise them in health. It vexes me that I should have to endure this sort of thing—my hands

Jim Lewis

won't let me sleep—and my vexation makes me jam my fingers against the mattress that much harder.

Childhood

I was very young, maybe six or seven, when I first experienced insomnia. It didn't strike me as a disability. I didn't even know it was unusual. A night in bed when sleep refused to come, was no worse than an overcast day when rain refused to come. A trap, of sorts, but no awful thing to bear. I would listen to the radio by my bed, to music or talk shows, which were much less bumptious than they are now. They were soothing, the conversation of the sleepless, and something like reasoning took place, or at least debate. I grew up listening to anonymous, cranky old men holding forth, a rabbinate of the midnight air. Larry King was on the radio then, and two men named Barry—Farber and Gray—were on WMCA-AM; and very late at night, on a tiny FM station named WEVD (the call letters stood for Eugene V. Debs, the great American socialist) there was Leon Lewis, a man I adored because his show ran all the way through to dawn; because he was unfailingly kind, warm and quick to laugh; because we had the same last name; and because there were rumours (the fact that they couldn't be verified seemed to prove the whole point of radio) that he was black.

At the time, my father was a producer for a morning news show, and, until I was eight years old, he slept in shifts. He would go to bed at ten at night, wake up four hours later, and drive from our home in northern New Jersey to Manhattan, where he would prepare for the morning's broadcast. Then he would come home again at midday, go back to sleep for a second time, and be up by the time I came back home from school. In this way his sleep was divided almost perfectly in half, and posted on opposite ends of the day. He was just about as old then as I am now, and in retrospect it's almost unimaginable to me that he should have kept up this schedule, year after year. But back then it was just what my father did, and I wonder sometimes if it was this early example that convinced me that sleep is so frangible.

Every so often my father would take my brother and me in to work with him. We would go to bed at our normal hour, wake up in darkness, climb sleepily into the car with him, and make our way

218

through the Lincoln Tunnel, to emerge again in Manhattan at night. The studios were located on Tenth Avenue, and my father would point out people on the street at that incredible hour: the Night People, he called them. This was 1971 or so—a few years before the movie *Taxi Driver*, and the city was just like that: garish, blurry, bruise-coloured. At the time I had no idea who any of the Night People were, what they were doing, or why they were doing it at three in the morning. I don't remember them being especially furtive, or gaudy, or boisterous, or lost, or anything else that I would now associate with being awake at that hour. They were simply the Night People, and as I lay awake in bed throughout the following weeks, I thought about them a lot, and wanted to be one of them the way other kids I knew wanted to be rock stars or astronauts.

Lullabies

As soon as we're born we're invited to sleep. Next to milk it's the pre-eminent mutual goal of mothers and infants, and when things go wrong the level of suffering is extraordinary. I've seen otherwise solid marriages almost end because of a sleepless baby, and parents fail their jobs for coming in stumbling, wasted and dull. A six-month-old who won't sleep can bring down a house, and there's nothing to be done about it.

The breast gives way to the bottle, and the bottle to the bowl, but the child's appetite for sleep doesn't shift objects quite so readily. There's no substitute for strong arms, a soft tone, and a gentle rhythm; a parent with a supply of lullabies is blessed, and so is the baby. You don't even need to have a good voice. I can't sing—by which I mean not just that I sing badly, but that what I do can't really be called singing at all. It's more like the noise I'd make if I were trying to convince someone to stop strangling me to death. Still, as long as I keep my voice soft, I, too, can sing a baby to sleep.

Dreams

So much has been written about dreams; I don't have much to add. I'm sure I have them, but I rarely remember them, and when I do, it's only for the first few hours of the morning, and then they're gone, blanched in the bright light of actual living, like film exposed to the sun.

It's true, I could keep my dreams by immediately writing them down, but if there's anything more boring than listening to someone describe what they dreamed the night before, it's going back over your own. The nocturnal fantasy of the world's most fascinating man or woman is less interesting than the dullest person's recitation of what they had for dinner the night before, and my own dreams are even less interesting than that. Besides, they're interruptions in the pure business of sleeping, the night's equivalent of cheap illustrations in a book of poems. Only amateurs sleep to dream.

Love

I sleep better when I'm sleeping with someone else, but she, unfortunately, does not. I snore like a beast, I gurgle and choke and stop breathing; I sprawl across the mattress. On the other hand—in my defence—I'm not selfish or greedy: I don't steal the blanket, or lash out from nightmares. In the land of Nod I am large and clumsy, but I'm affectionate without being needy, protective without being overbearing. I may even be a better man than I am in the land where I wake. Sleep, like alcohol, brings out an edition of the self, and as with alcohol, no one knows for sure whether it's a truer or purer version—one stripped of mistakes, misprints, and editorial amendments—or merely a different one.

We love watching our loved ones sleep. Most people assume that the pleasure comes from the apprehension of innocence, the years fallen away from the beloved's features, all self-protection erased, but I don't think so. For one thing, I've never had much use for innocence as a virtue—like, say, being three feet tall, it's perfectly appropriate for children, but a bizarre thing to want of an adult. Besides, I love to watch my dog sleep, too, and he chases cats in his dreams, which is more aggression than he can bothered with in real life. Nor is it anything as simple as the empathic delight that comes from watching the people we care about enjoying themselves. Seeing one's beloved dead drunk is seldom a pleasure, no matter how much pleasure he or she may be taking in it.

Watching someone sleep is a form of worship, an everyday awe, like the special regard some tribal societies have for schizophrenics, because they have access to some magical place, and are touched by a strange grace.

Then again… I remember a story I heard a few years ago, about an acquaintance in New York who had moved into a new apartment with his girlfriend. They began renovating the place, but they were arguing a lot, and one night he gave up mid-fight and went to bed. 'We can talk about it in the morning,' he said. But she didn't want to go to bed, she was still angry, and something about watching him peacefully sleeping made her angrier and angrier, until at last she couldn't stand it any longer. So she got up from the bed, crossed the room, grabbed a two-by-four from where a workman had left it, came back and smashed him in the head with it. Then she set fire to the apartment, and then she walked out.

What happened after that I don't know. I saw the man a year or so later, and he seemed fine, if a bit dazed and fragile, as if the spine of his soul had been shattered and would never again be quite as whole or quite as strong. Not everyone loves to watch other people sleep.

Airplanes

Airplane travel is the most infamous adversary of sleep, especially if the trip is one of those all-day, multiple-time-zone voyages, which pluck you from the face of the clock and deposit you at some distant moment in some faraway landscape. If you're flying economy, you'll be imprisoned in a dusty upholstered corner with your face smeared against the glass like a cartoon cat wedged into a cartoon bottle, you'll be utterly dependent on the flight crew, and a few hours of shut-eye will be your only possible deliverance.

There are people, I know, who can sleep just about anywhere, in any position—there are those who can grab a nap on a roller coaster. But I can only sleep sprawled out on my stomach; nothing else works. Sitting upright, or even reclining on my back, renders me absolutely awake, or at least suspends me—as yet another hour goes by and we're passing over Kamchatka—somewhere between alertness and exhaustion, hallucinating that the ice fields below are sheets on a hotel bed that I'll never, ever reach.

The ability to nod off is the ultimate exercise of freedom. The choice not to be there: no wonder human-rights groups condemn sleep deprivation as a form of prisoner abuse. For almost every waking malaise—discomfort, depression, boredom—sleep is an

221

escape. No one is bored by dreaming; no one is dissatisfied while sleeping. To keep a prisoner awake, then, is to compound the confinement of his body with the incarceration of his consciousness.

Flight attendants will insist that they are merely ensuring public safety and the smooth performance of whatever corporation they work for. Still, they may have more power over you, more legal right to limit your movement, than anyone else you'll ever encounter. You'd have roomier quarters and a better range of entertainment in a small-town jail cell on a Sunday night. An airplane is an almost perfect device for torture; and so you arrive at your destination, not just tired but insane.

Drugs

There's no sleep like an opium sleep. Or perhaps, more accurately, there's nothing quite so pleasant as opiate wakefulness, perched on the very edge of slumber. The indescribable sense of warmth and well-being, the dreamy, silky, creamy feeling, the profound restfulness... Well, I won't go into this any further. Every junkie's tale is the same, and none of them is very interesting, since the point of that kind of life is to make your days as dull as possible. Let me say this, though: It's a grim practical joke played by brain chemistry that opiates are so inescapably addictive, and so quickly lose the very plushness that draws you to them, the lusciousness of sleep distilled to its pearly essence.

Almost all recreational drugs, and most therapeutic ones, either induce or mimic sleep, or induce or mimic wakefulness. Thus, facing the dawn after a night of coke or speed is pretty much like facing the dawn after a restless night tossing on your mattress. The light is a pale, mungy green, and so is your skin. The whole world is shuddering back into view, with faint, twittering noises and the smell of car exhaust. Ordinary people, whom you envy and hate, are just now getting up to go to work. The ass end of your night is a new beginning to them. Their normality is grotesque: your prodigality is disgusting. People pay money to feel this way.

But there are no pills to make you feel like you're in love, or rich, or virtuous. There's nothing to cure, say, wanderlust, or to simulate the experience of a good loud laugh. When you get down to it, most of what we have are uppers and downers—the antipodes around

which our lives are arranged. It's a form of Manichaeism: some say
the world is fashioned out of the tensions between good and evil,
some say everything is made out of positive or negative electrical
charge, some say history is made out of the conflicts of wealth and
poverty. I say God made his own opinion clear when he first divided
day from night, and thereby wakefulness from sleep.

Sleep Lab

This is where you go when your doctor determines that your sleep
has entered the category of disorder, that you slumber the way people
with emphysema breathe, and something has to be done or else you'll
die. —Die? It seems melodramatic, like dying from indigestion, or a
bad haircut. Isn't this the hypochondria of contemporary life?
Everything is a pathology, even insomnia; it's as if restedness was our
birthright, rather than a blessing. Still, in the vast statistical labyrinth
of modern medicine, it's well known that people with sleeping
disorders live briefer lives than those without (though they're
probably awake for about the same number of hours), and the
economics of it are clear enough that insurance companies will pay
to have these things corrected. Your wakefulness is no longer the
metaphysical burden it once was, no longer the ruminative midnight
of Fitzgerald or Proust: it's a well-researched medical anomaly with
carefully charted financial consequences, and every dream is
redeemable in dollars.

The sleep lab is a miserable place, the first stop on the way to a
cure hardly less distressing than the disease itself. The one I went to
looked like any other doctor's office: bright fluorescent lights in the
waiting room, a brisk and efficient staff. The fact that I arrived at
ten at night was disorienting, but not bizarre. The creepy part was
the room where the nurse led me, which had been made up to look
like a cheap but clean motel room: polyester bedspread, flimsy night
table, plastic lamp, and a TV bolted into a bracket hanging from the
ceiling. She told me to make myself comfortable, but of course I
couldn't: there was such a profound gulf between the efficiency of
the office outside, and this make-believe bedroom. I thought of the
patients being attended to in adjacent rooms: it felt like I was in some
particularly clinical whorehouse, and I wondered if the other
bedrooms had been decorated very differently, as if in anticipation

of clients' fantasies—Tahitian grass-hut, suburban kitchen, Mexican prison—and if so, how and why they had decided that Motel 8 would work for me.

Then came the preparations: a cuff on my index finger to measure heartbeat and blood oxygen, and electrodes, at least a dozen of them, fastened to my arms, my legs, my chest, my scalp, with dollops of vaseline that I spent the next few days trying to wash off. There was a video camera perched in one corner of the room to monitor my night-time thrashing, and a microphone to record my snoring. Someone, I didn't know who, would be watching and listening to me all night long. The nurse brought me a plastic cup of water and a sleeping pill, and told me that I'd have to sleep on my back to keep from tearing the wires in which I was entangled. If I turned, she said, they would come in and wake me up. Then she left me alone.

I realized then what I had never noticed before: sleep is a kind of nineteenth-century activity. It belongs to the era of gaslights and chamber pots, not this super-modern world of cathode ray tubes and pulse-ox monitors. It's an activity for gentlemen and ladies; to climb into bed at night is to shake off a few centuries of technology. The trappings of sleep are bourgeois and mannerly, even if the activity itself is anarchic.

A miracle: I slept in that lab, for a little while anyway, though it felt like an anachronistic thing to do, and woke, just before dawn, having effortlessly generated hundreds of lines of data. The diagnosis, which I learned a week or so later in my doctor's office, was apnoea—involuntary cessation of breathing in my sleep, resulting in hundreds of micro-wakings throughout the night. The treatment is too crass to go into here; in any case, it doesn't seem to be working. Sleep is not something you diagnose and cure; it's something you seduce and abandon, night after night after night.

Patterns

Days unfold as days will, but night resolves itself into patterns, a sameness which shifts and changes somewhere deep, like the left hand in Bach.

In bed at 11. Up at 4.30. Asleep again at 5.15. Awake at 7.30.
In bed at 11. Awake at 6.30.

In bed at midnight. Up at 6.30. In bed again at 9. Wake at 10.30.
In bed at midnight. Up at 3. Up again at 4.30. Up again at 6.
Wake at 9.

In this way, weeks, months acquire a pattern, I want to say a
fashion, like the rise and fall of hemlines or heels, something with a
will of its own, in which individuals are only participants. That was
the season I saw daybreak every morning; that was the season I
couldn't concentrate after dinner. Often I feel as if I'm not engaging
in sleep so much as my sleep is engaging in me.

Moon
I know I'm not the first to say that the moon is the most beautiful
thing in the world. The most feminine thing, too; not because its light
is reflected, but because it's so pale. To an insomniac like me the
moon is La Belle Dame sans Merci, it causes shivers and sweats, it
disdains me and I suffer.

Waking
I own an alarm clock but I never use it; I'm not even sure what noise
it makes when it goes off. I'd rather sleep through anything than be
woken by a bell or a beeping, or worst of all, by some cheerful voice
on the radio. I read somewhere that Plains Indians would make sure
they woke early on battle mornings by drinking an excess of water
the night before. This seems both civil and reasonable, if you have
a battle to fight. If not: 'When I dance, I dance,' Montaigne says in
'Of Experience', 'When I sleep, I sleep.' And I'll wake when I wake.

I've heard that there are people who wake 'refreshed'. The idea
is absurd. Sleeping is no more a means to being awake than being
awake is a preparation for sleeping, and so the transition between
the two ought to be slow and cumbersome. It's like passing over the
border into China; the hours of bureaucracy, the delays, the checks,
the questions, all reinforce to you the fact that you're about to enter
some land where things are not done as they are in the land you're
leaving. You don't speed carelessly into China, waving cheerfully to
the guards from the driver's seat of your convertible sports car. I can't
wake refreshed, and I don't quite trust anyone who can.

The only pleasure daybreak brings is that of waking with morning

225

wood, that lingering throb of sleep's final touch. Make fun if you want to, but it's an uncompromised delight, like the last kiss of a first date—a kind of gratuity or lagniappe, a gift, and a sign that sleep is good, since it leaves you with this. It's the only part of waking that I can endorse.

Naps

There's a period between four and six in the evening when the day seems to hang, motionless and idle in the air. The work day is done, and your mind needs the kind of rest that reading won't provide; the evening news hasn't yet come on TV, it is too early to start thinking about what to have for dinner. The sun has lowered, its rays are reclining, the light is long, inviting. This is the perfect time for a nap, and I've taken one almost every day of my adult life. Here are the rules I've discovered.

It's important, if possible, not to nap in bed, since you can't always stop yourself from falling into a too-deep sleep and waking an hour or two later. Long naps are a disaster; you never quite wake up from them, and you'll never get back to sleep that night, either, so you'll spend the rest of the evening in torpid dread. Stay out of bed: napping on the couch is much better, or even on the floor, or in the passenger seat of a car while someone else is driving. A blanket may be used, but not bed sheets; and you must wear more clothing than you do at night: if you sleep naked, some form of underwear is obligatory for napping; if you sleep topless, a shirt; and if you sleep in pyjamas, I suppose you have to nap with your shoes on. You may drool on the pillow, or on your sleeve if that's where your head's resting. For some reason, napping with the radio on is less satisfying then napping with the television on. If you own a dog, he should be in the same room as you: dogs are experts in the art of dozing, and man and beast nod off twice as well together as either does alone. You may freely snore in your own living room, but if you nap in public, be prepared to bolt awake with a dazed and foolish expression, and find other people staring at you.

Why are long naps so much more disorienting than a full night's sleep? Your senses are so slow to come and get you. They dawdle and arrive at different times. Your hearing is the first to come alive again: the sound of someone entering the room, the murmur of conversation outside the door, a police siren passing below. Then you see where you are, you're on the couch, you're in your living room, but your body is still asleep, you're still breathing like a patient under gas, and there's a very brief moment of panic—paralysed!—but no, this arm's working, the other arm, you pull your knees up and groan softly, blink your eyes, smack your lips, sigh. Everything worldly is as you left it; only the clock has turned forward, and you have changed exactly that much.

Men tend to nap more often than women—or so it seems from the surveys I've conducted among my friends and acquaintances. If it's true for the population as a whole, I can't explain it. Maybe it's a matter of metabolism, maybe of conditioning, maybe simply of opportunity. Whatever it is, I suspect it's the same cause that makes men fall asleep immediately after sex, while women lie awake; but I don't know. Like most differences between men and women, it may be inherent, or it may be contingent, or it may not be real at all, so I'll just mention it here and move on.

Tired

Sleep is gravity. Sleep is the home that waits at the bottom of consciousness. This morning I woke at around four a.m. I don't know why this happens, but it happens most nights. I'm pitched into this peculiar hour, too late for most things (the bars are closed, the TV is all infomercials), and too early for the rest (the morning newspaper hasn't been delivered yet, and no one I know is awake). In fact I don't know whether it's still Wednesday, or Thursday by now, and it's too faint an hour for reading or writing. Nothing sticks.

Trapped, a few years ago, in a black-dog depression, I remember walking around repeating the phrase *I'm so unhappy* under my breath. When I wasn't saying it, I was thinking it. *I'm so unhappy. I'm so unhappy.* It was something I was helpless to stop, and in fact I was often unconscious of it. Then I would snap to, overhear myself murmuring this little phrase, and be that much more miserable. Much the same thing happens when I can't sleep: I find the sentence *I'm so tired, I'm so tired* running through my head, until the words themselves exhaust me.

To be tired without being sleepy is one of the world's fundamental paradoxes, like the habit some people have of only falling in love

Jim Lewis

with those who are unavailable, or the existence of evil in a universe
governed by a benevolent god.

Envoi

My affection for sleeping is so complete that it's changed the way I
think about the finitude of life itself. Just mentioning it makes me
uneasy; I don't want to tempt fate, and I'm superstitious enough to
believe that you shouldn't discuss these things casually. Still, I think
about it often enough, and I might as well say it: given how
wonderful sleep is, imagine how pleasurable death must be.　　□

GRANTA

HOW TO STOP YOUR MOTHER-IN-LAW FROM DROWNING

DROWNING

Richard Beard

How to Stop Your Mother-in-Law from Drowning

This is one of those stories about she and you. She is the mother-in-law. You are the man who duped her daughter, or the woman who ensnared her son. Or stole or deceived or sidetracked, or diminished or corrupted or hardened, depending on how stereotyped either you or she find the relationship to be.

Two women appeared before King Solomon, dragging between them a reluctant young man. 'This good-for-nothing promised to marry my daughter,' said one.
'No! He promised to marry my daughter,' said the other.
'Bring me an axe,' the king said. 'I shall chop the youngster into two pieces, and you shall each receive a half.'
'Sounds good to me,' said the first lady.
'Oh, your Highness,' protested the second. 'Don't spill innocent blood. Let the other woman's daughter marry him.'
The wise king had heard enough. 'This man must marry the first lady's daughter,' he proclaimed.
'But she was willing to have him hewn in two!'
'Indeed,' said wise King Solomon. 'She is therefore the true mother-in-law.'

The she is a woman, and always more than a woman: a mother. In this case, the you is a son-in-law, but you can also be a woman, a daughter-in-law. It's no easier either way, because the problem of the mother-in-law is universal, and universally thought to be funny.

Abu El Abed's mother-in-law died. Abu Staeif went to offer his condolences and ask him how it had happened.
Abu El Abed: She was leaning on the balcony when she flipped over and—
Abu Staeif: She hit the ground and died?
Abu El Abed: No, she hit the electricity cable and—
Abu Staeif: She got electrocuted?
Abu El Abed: No, she got deflected to our neighbour's swimming pool and—
Abu Staeif: She drowned?
Abu El Abed: No, she hit the diving board and bounced all the way back to the balcony intact—

Abu Staief (confused): How did your mother-in-law die then?
Abu El Abed: I grabbed my rifle and shot her.

Why was El Abed so determined to see her off? What made her so intolerable? For me, it was her intrusive anxiety. My mother-in-law had no doubt that anxiety was the correct response to life. Her timidity was therefore very assured, almost aggressive. She seldom liked the gist of the weather, or an undated yoghurt, or the Albanian look of a waiter (they spit in the soup, you know). She insisted on locked top-floor windows and boiled meat and toilets buffed with Windowlene.

Doctor: I'm sorry to say that your mother-in-law has had a heart attack.
You: That's impossible!
Doctor: What do you mean that's impossible?
You: She doesn't have a heart!

She was often fluttering with terror because the world in which her only daughter was making her way was full of haste and recklessness and danger. At first, this militant vulnerability could seem amusing, an ongoing joke. I used to tease her by arriving in T-shirt and shorts on my motorcycle, or by preparing conspicuously for a swim in the local fast-flowing river. She'd plead with me not to risk my life, and I'd laugh and go anyway. Back safe and sound, I'd apologize. Then spend the rest of the day intercepting her unquestioning motherly love as it flooded across rooms at her child. Her only child. I'd attach to that certain love my own less conclusive emotions, and feel them nourished.

Even so, we never managed a lasting compromise. Taking her daughter on the bike became the most solemn secret of the engagement. The roads were lethal. People get killed. Of course, I nodded, I'd never dream of riding us over the Alps to Lake Como where the water is cold and blue.

'You hear terrible stories.'
'You do.'
'Quite dreadful.'
She simply couldn't help her anxiety on our behalf, while I preferred to believe that nothing could touch us because we were young and special. And I was doing the driving.

How to Stop Your Mother-in-Law from Drowning

Later, and I can't say exactly when (perhaps when I sold the bike), it stopped being funny.

Mother-in-law: If you don't like me, why do you take me on holidays?
Son-in-law: So I don't have to kiss you goodbye.

After several years of marriage, you go on holiday with your husband or wife's parents. In this case, counting the children, that makes four against two. Or four against one, because my father-in-law remained a figure in shadow. In his favour, I hoped it was reassuring and even inspiriting nearly always to be in the right. To live for years and travel for miles with someone whose next idea or instinct was always more ridiculous than his own. Must make a man feel needed, I'd reasoned, and useful. So then, four against one, though my wife couldn't be expected to take sides against her own mother (three against one), and the children loved their grandparents. Which made it one against one, single combat, in July 2003 on the Atlantic coast of France.

We were arriving from different directions by road, because she distrusted air travel. She also avoided motorways, for reasons of speed, and it once took us two days to drive safely from Paris to Strasbourg. She was a very attentive driver. Leaning forward over the wheel, she rarely even blinked.

Three friends were discussing the possibility of sudden death.
'Everyone dies someday, but if only we knew when, we could make a better job of preparing ourselves.'
The friends nodded in agreement, and considered what they'd do with two weeks left to live.
'Go out and have as much sex as possible,' said one, and the others murmured in agreement.
'Give all my possessions to worthy causes,' said another.
The last of the friends then spoke up. 'For those two weeks, I'd stay on the Atlantic coast of France with my mother-in-law.'
The others were puzzled by this answer. 'Why would you do that?'
'Because,' you say, 'It would be the longest two weeks of my life.'

Richard Beard

More than once, as we moved fast down the bright straight roads
of northern France, I flirted with disaster by driving on the wrong
side of the road. I was remembering childhood holidays with my own
parents, strictly no in-laws, when these *routes nationales* were
shaded by glorious avenues of plane trees, providing shade and a
dappled vanishing point. Most of the trees are gone now, in the
interests of safety. 'Make an effort,' the daughter of my mother-in-
law said. 'The two of you may even get on.'

We'd never physically fought, though I feel she sometimes wanted
to hit me. Mostly, we avoided looking at each other, and failed to
communicate directly for days on end, especially around Christmas.
I'd occasionally flounced out of a room, apparently to stop myself
doing something I'd regret. Of course we didn't get on well. If we
had, it wouldn't have been funny.

> Murphy's mother-in-law was walking round the farm, when a mule
> attacked her and she died. Five hundred married men turned up at
> the funeral, and Father O'Toole said to Murphy, 'I never realized
> your mother-in-law was so popular.' Murphy said, 'Father, they're
> not here for the funeral. They've come to buy the mule.'

We were involved in a universal conflict. The earliest recorded
mother-in-law jibe is Juvenal's from the first century AD, showing
that along with hairdressing and a liking for fresh flowers, the tension
between you and her is a feature of every culture at all times. It's
inevitable, biological. It's human nature.

Abu El Abed and Murphy (and Aaron and Piotr and Li Po Chu)
fantasize the early death of their mother-in-law to put an end to the
otherwise endless contention over who's right, what's best, and,
ultimately, the correct way to live. The universal complaint is that
she thinks you're not good enough for her child. If you have any
self-knowledge, and you adore the person you married, you'll know
she's right. This makes the situation worse. On this one vital point
you can agree, but that doesn't mean you need to be reminded. You
therefore disagree about how to roast a chicken, the definition of
smart-casual, and the itinerary for a visit to historic La Rochelle
(which you didn't want to make in the first place and, lest anyone
forget, you're actually paying for).

How to Stop Your Mother-in-Law from Drowning

She and you squabble, fall out, and we were no different. Before long, disagreeing in itself became a habit: the date of the wedding, where to live, the children's names. She didn't like the covers of the books I read, or the boots I wore around the house. I didn't like the way she ate with her mouth open, usually while speaking, as if there was never time for considerate chewing. She might choke before she'd get the words out, when what she had to say, invariably, was death and disaster. In reply, I could indulge my instinct that nothing I said or did would matter very much. I could therefore say what I thought. She would always be my mother-in-law and she would always visit. Later, I'd gripe in private to my wife, I'd whine and roll my eyes, but not too much, because that's not a good idea in any relationship.

You're trying to be adult, having babies, working hard, moving into the attempted universe of marriage. It's important not to be childish, and instead to behave as if you know and are more than you once were. Back in the days when you were still a child, say, and visibly needed a mother. Then this woman arrives, she eats with her mouth open, she is present, and she is all mother, even more so than a natural mother, your own mother. She is related to you entirely by her motherness, because how else would you have met? What other reason do you have for keeping in touch? You've shared no experiences, nor seen her in any other context save as the mother of the mother of your children. In a charmed future, she may one day become the mother of the mother of the mother of your grandchildren. My own mum can't do that, however hard she tries, however many cakes she bakes.

> 'I don't dislike all mothers-in-law,' you say. 'I like yours much better than I like mine.'

You have loads of excuses, and some of them may even be reasonable. You love her daughter or her son, who is good and strong. They must be, because you love them. So how can the mother be so difficult? And if she *is* impossible (and tremulous too), maybe your wife or husband isn't good and strong, except by some miracle which defies genetic inheritance. In the absence of miracles, you're therefore living with an impostor who is in fact aggressively timid, and who will one day speak while eating.

Richard Beard

Try another possibility: no one is lovable all the time, especially not the person you married. You may not want this to be true, but bring her into it, bring in your mother-in-law, and it's a safe way of deflecting the temporary dislike you feel for your wife, your husband. Transfer the annoying characteristics to your mother-in-law, and if this positive displacement works for you, then thank God she's still there. This could be what mothers-in-law are for.

The village where we'd rented a house was supposed to be neutral territory, safe and slow, the only possible irritation the buzz of fourteen-year-olds on their mopeds lapping the church and the *boulanger* via the nearest *route départementale*. In the corner of the village cafe the pendulum of a tall clock tocked slowly, perhaps too slowly, because we soon lapsed into familiar stand-offs and disputes, and a running breakfast-time bicker about whether to finish the old bread before starting on the fresh. We ate many meals without once looking each other in the eye, while my wife remained good and strong by a miracle which defied genetic inheritance.

There were some problems with the house: it faced on to a main road (without pavement), and it was just conceivably feasible to walk out of the door into traffic. There was a small garden in the back with an iron table-and-chairs set, and a rusted metal spike protruding from the grass of the lawn. I spent an evening trying to dig it out. It wouldn't budge. I spent the next morning covering it over, burying it beneath a mound of earth and sand.

The more obvious danger that summer was the sea, because our two children were young and submersible. The ocean, on the other hand, was ancient and merciless.

'Don't worry about the sea,' my wife said, giving her mum a hug. 'Enjoy the beach.'

I bought a flimsy plastic dinghy, of the kind often swept out on the tide, because it scared the living daylights out of her. Then I took the kids for rides while she looked on, inches from the last wave-break in her billowing flower-pattern sundress. She was agitated, terrified, a non-swimmer poised to save us all, and she grimaced every time the inflatable buckled on an incoming wave. It felt too late to be angry. What once used to astound me—the fear, the ineffectiveness, the kind heart—suddenly looked like old age. I started feeling sorry for her, not only at the beach but in the

How to Stop Your Mother-in-Law from Drowning

supermarket at L'Aiguillon, where she hunted packets and jams like a predator, shoulders hunched, nerves trembling to the underrated menace of faulty trollies and overpriced dairy products.

The secret was to watch her when she didn't know she was being watched. I'd distanced her from her only child, just by one step, but from the centre. No wonder we should tussle, bicker, fight. It was for love, jealous love.

On her last night at the house, we celebrated our defeat of life's many dangers by cooking a special meal. We then stayed up late disagreeing about Muslims. She insisted we promise never to live in Paris, where Muslim Arabs would rob and mug us, or worse. Adhering to the principle of disagreement, keeping her up much later than was usual, I couldn't help but goad and provoke her. What, *all* Muslims? *All* of them?

It was easy to forget that earlier in the day I'd been pushing the flimsy dinghy with the two kids in it, up to my chin in the Atlantic, deeper than I'd wanted to be. Standing in her sundress on the shore, she was waving or beckoning, pleading with us to come back in, come back safely, and I'd suddenly tired of this unwinnable squabble. I'd wanted to escape its predictability, and spying on her from behind the dinghy, I'd thought the trick—no, the achievement—would be to look at our parents like we look at our children. With the same love, the same gratitude, and the same precious attention to detail.

At the table later that evening she was tired, flagging, but stubborn about Paris. It took so long and came out so garbled because she couldn't care less about Muslims. She was saying, in her ardent but indirect way: *Be careful. Be very careful. Not just here and now, but wherever you go and always. I love you.*

The tendons in her neck stood out, and she was so anxious for us that she was suffering agonies, all the time. Her complexion was green with worry, and her eyes darted constantly left and right. She loved us, she loved us so much, and I wished just once I'd shown some understanding. From now on, I vowed to myself, from now on. Let her live, exist as more than a mother-in-law. Let the poor woman surface and breathe.

Q. How do you stop your mother-in-law from drowning?
A. Take your foot off her head.

If not in her own bed, or peacefully in the conservatory of a cool green nursing home, then your mother-in-law might go something like this: in a burgundy Peugeot 305, on a straight stretch of French road, somewhere near the ugly provincial town of Niort.

We went to bed late and on bad terms, and woke up irritable. At our last breakfast, she chewed yesterday's bread, because it was there (and with her mouth open). I ate the fresh bread, because it was there (mouth closed, eyes averted). I can now see both sides of this argument.

We kissed goodbye, unlike in the joke. Then I stood in the doorway for a long time waving away her car, which proceeded slowly to the nearest junction, where it stopped. My father-in-law looked back and waved. My mother-in-law kept her eyes on the road. I went back indoors before they moved off again.

The next morning we were on the same road, in shock, worn out, with everything happening slowly and the day taking forever. About seventy kilometres inland, at the Mercure Hotel in Niort, we found her husband, my father-in-law, in grief on under the trees on the terrace.

I wanted to help, because the last thing you want to do is look in the mirror and see your own dishonesty. You therefore do the driving to the gendarmerie, the *mairie*, the *pompes funèbres*. The policemen said there was little point visiting the crash site, especially with two small children, and in the heat. They said the sequence of events was clear from the markings and scars on the road.

We went anyway, and stared inexpertly at the metallic gouges and black smudges of rubber. It was so hot in the middle of the empty straight road that the tarmac stuck to our shoes.

There was a bang, my father-in-law said, white-faced, not always making much sense. I was reading from the Michelin, he said, telling her about the church at Poitiers, so I had my head down and there was a bang and my first reaction was to shout out what have you done *now*?

She'd fallen asleep at the wheel, drifted across the road. The chances against it were phenomenal, like any punchline, but a lorry was at that moment coming in the other direction. She must have woken up before impact, an instant before the bonnet shuddered against the leading edge of the lorry's trailer. The Peugeot careened back on to its own side of the road, skidding round on itself, sliding backwards, ending up sizzling and crackling on the smooth grass next to tree-stumps which had once edged an avenue.

The driver of the lorry was called M. Clochard. The first medic to reach the car was Dr Camus, who examined her as she slumped behind the wheel. Her fingers were no longer closing, even faintly, as a sign that she was hearing, that something was understood. Already at the roadside, while she was still in the car, the doctor admitted or announced it was hopeless.

When the news reached us the night before, my wife had fallen instantly to the floor, crouching on her knees, head clenched tightly between her elbows. She cried out for her mother, with so much love, and love lost, which is grief. There was the past, and all its detail, but also the love lost from the future, the years of mothering and grand-mothering unmothered, the hand-holding unheld. The loss, too, of a chance to repay some of that unpriced, unconditional mother's love: hot meals during the last days in her own home, a room at the front of the house, daily care and life-saving interventions.

And through my wife, crying out, rocking in despair on the floor, I felt the opposite of the immense rolling mother's love I had once intercepted. Grief can suck love away and out of the world, and it's all you can do to try and haul it back.

We went to the recovery garage to look at the car. The mechanics in their oil-company overalls stopped whatever they were doing and stared. They knew who we were, and which of their wrecks my father-in-law had survived unscathed. The Peugeot was a spectacular mess, dropped in a corner of the yard with the driver's side detached and dumped on the roof. My wife's father put his head inside and picked up a navy-blue cardigan with gold buttons. It was heavy with blood. He dropped it back on the floor.

All that day I drove carefully, obsessively, like she'd always wanted. From the back seat, my son asked his mother how you spell *dead*. He wanted to know, quite insistently, what happens when you die. As if this was what mothers were for, to answer questions such as these.

M. Terrasson of the *pompes funèbres* directed us to a six-room mortuary at the road end of a small industrial estate. Shamed by death, caught out by it before I could make amends, I stumbled into the familiar formulas, like obstacles.

Q. Why did you go to see your mother-in-law's body?
A. To check that she was dead.

She was unlike herself, expressionless. The left side of her face had been rebuilt and heavily made up with brown foundation. I'd never seen her with her head still, or her eyes closed. Nor with her mouth shut, top lip stretched tight over her teeth. This was not how she was. This was some kind of joke.

Q. Why didn't you recognize your mother-in-law when she was laid out at the mortuary?
A. She had her mouth shut.

She was dressed and had her shoes on. The kids couldn't understand that. If she's resting in peace, why is she lying down and seemingly asleep but still wearing her shoes?

It took more than a week to organize and route and pay for the body to leave France, by which time letters of condolence were backing up on the mat. My father-in-law said that some of them left him cold. Others, unexpectedly, moved or consoled him. I read some of the cards, full of her beauty and warmth and serenity, and I asked my father-in-law which ones left him colder, the formulaic messages or the exaggerated ones.

'None of them exaggerate,' he said.

There was a funeral, in a beautiful cemetery overlooking a lake. A speech was made in German, *Sie war eine gute Mensch*. Her clothes, her coats, her shoes were picked up by a grey-haired lady from one of the Protestant charities. The clothes have since been distributed in Africa, so she lives on under cloudless skies, her cardigans and sundresses parading through the bustle of African markets.

She lives on in memory, and in the photos we keep of her around the house, and in certain physical mannerisms of the children, who are sometimes reckless. I watch anxiously from a distance, thinking that it's vitally important to be careful. Be very careful. Not just here and now, but wherever you go and always. More than that. Recognize the outright need to value every moment of being of the people you love. It seems an unbearable duty, an oppressive charge, and I try to keep it from the children. I don't want to make them anxious, as she was, knowing that however much you value each moment it's not enough, never enough, when the shock comes, the astonishing end. ☐

In memory of Christiane Nagy (1940–2003)

GRANTA

WHEN THERE IS
TALK OF 1945

Ryszard Kapuscinski

TRANSLATED FROM THE POLISH BY
KLARA GLOWCZEWSKA

German Luftwaffe over Poland

Total war has a thousand fronts; during such a war, everyone is at the front, even if they never lie in a trench or fire a single shot. When I go back in memory to those days, I realize, not without a certain surprise, that I remember the beginning of the war better than its end. Its onset is clearly fixed for me in time and place. I can conjure up its image without difficulty because it has retained all its colours, all its emotional intensity. It starts with my suddenly noticing one day, in the azure sky of a summer's ending (and the sky in September 1939 was wondrously blue, without a single cloud), somewhere very, very high up, twelve glittering silver points. The entire bright, lofty dome of the sky fills with a dull, monotonous rumble, unlike anything I've ever heard before. I am seven years old, I am standing in a meadow in eastern Poland, and I am staring at the points that are barely moving across the sky. Suddenly, there's a dreadful bang close-by, at the edge of the forest. I hear bombs exploding. It is only later that I learn they are bombs, for at this moment I do not yet know that there is such a thing as a bomb; the very notion is foreign to me, a child from the deepest provinces who had never even listened to a radio or gone to the movies, who didn't know how to read or write, who had never heard of wars and deadly weapons. I see gigantic fountains of earth spraying up into the air. I want to run towards this extraordinary spectacle which stuns and fascinates me, because, having as yet no wartime experiences, I am unable to connect into a single chain of cause and effect those shining silver planes, the thunder of the bombs, the plumes of earth flying up to the height of the trees, and the danger of imminent death. I start to run there, towards the forest and the falling and exploding bombs, but a hand grabs me from behind and throws me to the ground. 'Lie still!' I hear my mother's shaking voice. 'Don't move!' And I remember my mother, as she presses me close to her, saying something I don't understand and which I want to ask her about later. She is saying, 'There's death over there, child.'

It's night and I'm sleepy, but I am not allowed to sleep; we must run, we must escape. Where to, I don't know. But I do understand that flight has suddenly become some sort of higher necessity, a new form of life, because everyone is fleeing. All the highways, roads, even country paths are full of wagons, carriages, and bicycles; full of

Ryszard Kapuscinski

bundles, suitcases, bags, buckets; full of terrified and helplessly wandering people. Some are making their way to the east, others to the west, still others to the north and the south. They run in all directions, circle about, collapse from exhaustion, fall asleep anywhere they can, and then, having caught their breath for a moment, they summon what's left of their strength and start once again their confused and endless journey.

I am supposed to hold my little sister tightly by the hand. We can't get lost, my mother warns. But I sense, even without her saying it, that the world has suddenly become dangerous, foreign and evil, and that one must be on one's guard. I walk with my sister next to the horse-drawn wagon; it is a simple wooden cart lined with hay, and high up on the hay, on a linen sheet, lies my grandfather. He is paralysed and cannot move. When an air raid starts, the panicked crowd, until then patiently trudging along, dives for the shelter of the ditches, hides in the bushes, drops down in the potato fields. On the empty, deserted road only the wagon remains, and on it my grandfather. He sees the planes coming towards him, sees them abruptly descending, sees them taking aim at the abandoned wagon, sees the fire of the on-board guns, hears the roar of the machines over his head. When the planes vanish, we return to the wagon and mother wipes my grandfather's perspiring face. Sometimes there are air raids several times a day. After each one, sweat trickles down my grandfather's exhausted face.

We find ourselves in an increasingly bleak landscape. There is smoke along the distant horizon, we pass empty settlements, lonely, burned-out houses. We pass battlefields strewn with abandoned implements of war, bombed out railway stations, overturned cars. It smells of gunpowder, of burnt things, of rotting meat. We encounter dead horses everywhere. The horse—a large, defenceless animal—doesn't know how to hide; during a bombardment it stands motionless, awaiting death. There are dead horses in the roads, in ditches, in the fields a bit further out. They lie there with their legs up in the air, as if shaking their hooves at the world. I don't see dead people anywhere; they are quickly buried. Only the horses—black, bay, piebald, chestnut—lie where they stood, as if this were not a human war but a war of horses; as if it were they who had waged among themselves a battle to the death and were its only victims.

A cold and hard winter arrives. Under difficult circumstances, one feels the cold more keenly; the chill is more penetrating. Winter can be just another season, a waiting for spring; but now winter is a disaster, a catastrophe. That first winter of the war is truly bitter. In our apartment the stoves are cold and the walls covered with thick white frost. There is nothing to burn; there is no fuel to buy, and it's too dangerous to steal any. It's death if you're caught filching coal or wood. Human life is worth little now, no more than a lump of coal or a piece of kindling. We have nothing to eat. Mother stands motionless for hours at the window, staring out. You can see people gazing out at the street like this in many windows, as if they were counting on something, waiting for something. I roam around the yards with a group of boys, neither playing nor explicitly hunting for something to eat; that would mean hope and then disappointment. Sometimes the smell of warm soup wafts through a door. When that happens one of my friends, Waldek, sticks his nose into the crack and begins feverishly to inhale the odour and to rub his stomach with delight, as if he were sitting at a sumptuously laid table. A moment later he grows sad again, and listless.

One day we hear that they are going to be giving away candy in a store near the square. We immediately line up—a string of cold and hungry children. It's the afternoon already, and getting dark. We stand all evening in the freezing temperatures, then all night and all the following day. We stand huddled together, hugging each other for a little bit of warmth, so as not to freeze. Finally the store opens, but instead of candy we each get an empty metal tin that once used to contain fruit drops. Weak, stiff from the cold and yet, at that moment, happy, I carry home my booty. It is valuable because a residue of sugar still remains on the inside walls of the can. My mother heats up some water, pours it into the can, and we have a hot, slightly sweet beverage: our only nourishment that day.

Then we are on the road again, travelling westwards from our town, Pinsk, because my mother has heard that our father is living in a village outside Warsaw. He was captured at the front, escaped, and is now, we think, teaching children in a small country school. When those of us who were children during the war recall that time and say 'father' or 'mother', we forget, because of the solemnity of those words, that our mothers were young women and our fathers were young men and that they desired each other strongly, missed each other terribly, and wanted to be together. And so my mother sold everything in the house, rented a wagon, and we set off to search for our father. We found him by accident. Riding through the village called Sieraków, my mother suddenly cries out to a man crossing the road: 'Dziudek!' From that day we live together in a tiny room without water or electricity. When it grows dark, we go to bed, because there aren't even candles. Hunger has followed us here from Pinsk. I search constantly for something to eat—a crust of bread, a carrot, anything. One day, father, having no other recourse, tells his class: 'Children, whoever wants to come to school tomorrow must bring one potato.' Father didn't know how to trade, didn't know how to do business and received no salary, so he decided he had only one option: to ask his students for a few potatoes. Half the class don't show up the next day. Some children bring half a potato, others a quarter. A whole potato is an enormous treasure.

Next to my village lies a forest, and in that forest, near a settlement called Palmira, is a clearing. In this clearing SS men carry out executions. At first, they shoot at night and we are woken up by the dull, repetitive sound of gunfire. Later, they do it also by day. They transport the condemned in enclosed, dark-green trucks, with the firing squad bringing up the rear of the convoy in a truck without a covering.

The firing squad always wear long overcoats, as if a long overcoat belted at the waist were an indispensable prop in the ritual of murder. When such a convoy passes by, we, the village children, observe it from our hiding place in the roadside bushes. In a moment, behind the curtain of trees, something that we are forbidden to witness will begin. I feel a cold tremor running up and down my spine—I'm trembling. We wait for the sound of the salvos. There they are. Then come the individual shots. After a while the convoy returns to Warsaw. The SS men again bring up the rear. They are smoking cigarettes and talking.

At night the partisans come. They appear suddenly, their faces pressed against the window. I stare at them as they sit at the table, always excited by the same thought: that there is still time for them to die tonight, that they are marked by death. We could, of course, all die, but they embrace the possibility, confront it head on. They come one rainy night in autumn and talk to my mother in whispers (I haven't seen my father for a month now, and won't until the end of the war; he's in hiding). We get dressed quickly and leave: there is a round-up taking place nearby and entire villages are being deported to the camps. We flee to Warsaw, to a designated hiding place. I see a large city for the first time: trams, multi-storey buildings, big stores. Then we are in the countryside again in yet another village, this time on the far bank of the Vistula. I can't remember why we went. I remember only walking once again next to a horse-drawn wagon and hearing the sand of the warm country road sifting through the wheels' wooden spokes.

All through the war I dream of shoes. To have shoes. But how? What must one do to get a pair? In the summer I walk barefoot, and the skin of my soles is as tough as leather. At the start of the war father made me a pair of shoes out of felt, but he is not a shoemaker and the shoes look strange; besides, I've grown, and they are already too tight. I fantasize about a pair of big, strong, hobnailed shoes which make a distinctive noise as they strike the pavement. The fashion was then for high-topped boots; I could stare for hours at a good-looking pair. I loved the shine of the leather, loved listening to the crunching sound it made. But my dream of shoes was about more than beauty or comfort. A good, strong shoe was a symbol of prestige and power, a symbol of authority; a shoddy shoe was a sign of humiliation, the brand of a man who has been stripped of all dignity and condemned to a subhuman existence. But in those years all the shoes I lusted for trod past me in the street with indifference. I was left in my rough wooden clogs with their uppers of black canvas, to which I would sometimes apply a crude ointment in an unsuccessful attempt to impart a tiny bit of lustre.

Late in the war, I became an altar boy. My priest is the chaplain of a Polish Army field hospital. Rows of camouflaged tents stand hidden in a pine forest on the left bank of the Vistula. During the Warsaw Uprising, before the Russian army moved on the city in January 1945, an exhausting bustle reigns here. Ambulances speed in from the front lines, which rumble and smoke not far away. They bring

Ryszard Kapuscinski

the wounded, who are often unconscious and arranged hurriedly and in disarray one on top of the other, as if they were so many sacks of grain (only these sacks are dripping blood). The medics, themselves half dead from fatigue, take the wounded out, lay them on the grass, and then drench them with a fierce spray of cold water. Those that give some signs of life they carry into the operating tent (in front of this tent there is always a fresh pile of amputated arms and legs). Those that no longer move are brought to a large grave at the rear of the hospital. There, over that yawning tomb, I stand for hours next to the priest, holding his breviary and the cup with holy water. I repeat after him the prayer for the dead. 'Amen,' we say to each deceased, 'Amen,' dozens of times a day, but quickly, because somewhere beyond the woods the machinery of death is working non-stop. And then one day everything is suddenly quiet and empty—the ambulances stop coming, the tents disappear. The hospital has moved east. In the forest only the crosses remain.

And later? The passages above are a few pages from a book about my wartime years that I began to write and then abandoned. I wonder now what the book's final pages would have been like, its conclusion, its epilogue. What would have been written there about the end of the Second World War? Nothing, I think. I mean, nothing conclusive. Because in some fundamental sense, the war did not end for me in 1945, or at any time soon afterwards. In many ways, something of it endures in me still. For those who lived through it, war is never over, not in an absolute way. It is a truism that an individual dies only when the last person who knew and remembered him dies; that a human being finally ceases to exist when all the bearers of his memory depart this world. Something like this also happens with war. Those who went through it will never be free of it. It stays with them as a mental hump, a painful tumour, which even as excellent a surgeon as time will be unable to remove. Just listen to people who lived through a war when they sit down around a table of an evening. It doesn't matter what the first topics of conversation might be. There can be a thousand topics. But in the end there will be only one: reminiscences from the war. These people, even after years of peace, will superimpose war's images on each new reality, a reality with which they are unable to fully identify because it has to do with the present and they are possessed by the past, by the constant returning to what they lived through and how they managed to live through it, their thoughts an obsessively repeated retrospection.

But what does it mean, to think in the images of war? It means to see everything as existing at maximum tension, as reeking of cruelty and dread. Because wartime reality is a world of extreme, Manichaean reduction, which eliminates all intermediate hues, all things gentle and warm, and limits everything to an aggressive counterpoint, to black and white, to the most primal battle of two powers: the good and the evil. No one else on the battlefield! Only the good (in other words, us) and the evil (meaning everything that stands in our way, that opposes us, and which we force wholesale into the sinister category of the enemy). The image of war is imbued with the atmosphere of force, a nakedly physical force, grinding, smoking, constantly exploding, always on the attack, a force brutally expressed in every gesture, in every strike of a boot against pavement, of a rifle butt against a skull. Strength, in this universe, is the only criterion against which everything is measured—only the strong matter, their shouts, their fists. Every conflict is resolved not through compromise, but by destroying one's opponent. And all this plays itself out in a climate of exaltation, fury, and frenzy, in which we feel always stunned, tense, and threatened. We move in a world brimming with hateful stares, clenched jaws, full of gestures and voices that terrify.

For a long time I believed that this was the world, that this is what life looked like. It was understandable: The war years coincided with my childhood, and then with the beginnings of maturity, of rational thought, of consciousness. That is why it seemed to me that war, not peace, is the natural state. And so when the guns suddenly stopped, when the roar of exploding bombs could be heard no more, when suddenly there was silence, I was astonished. I could not fathom what the silence meant, what it was. I think that a grown-up confronted with that quiet could say: 'Hell is over. At last peace will return.' But I did not remember what peace was. I was too young for that; by the time the war was over, hell was all I knew.

Months passed, and war constantly reminded us of its presence. I continued to live in a city reduced to rubble, I climbed over mountains of debris, roamed through a labyrinth of ruins. The school

Ryszard Kapuscinski

that I attended had no floors, windows, or doors—everything had gone up in flames. We had no books or notebooks. I still had no shoes. War as trouble, as want, as burden, was still very much with me. I still had no home. The return home from the front is the most palpable symbol of war's end. *Tutti a casa!* But I could not go home. My home was now on the other side of the border, in another country called the Soviet Union. One day, after school, I was playing soccer with friends in a local park. One of them plunged into some bushes in pursuit of the ball. There was a tremendous bang and we were thrown to the ground: my friend was killed by a landmine. War thus continued to lay in wait for us; it didn't want to surrender. It hobbled along the streets supporting itself with wooden crutches, waving its empty shirtsleeves in the wind. It tortured at night those who had survived it, reminded them of itself in bad dreams.

But above all war lived on within us because for five years it had shaped our young characters, our psyches, our outlooks. It tried to deform and destroy them by setting the worst examples, compelling dishonourable conduct, releasing contemptible emotions. 'War,' wrote Boleslaw Micinski in those years, 'deforms not only the soul of the invader, but also poisons with hatred, and hence deforms, the souls of those who try to oppose the invader'. And that is why, he added, 'I hate totalitarianism because it taught me to hate.' Yes, to leave war behind meant to internally cleanse oneself, and first and foremost to cleanse oneself of hatred. But how many made a sustained effort in that direction? And of those, how many succeeded? It was certainly an exhausting and long process, a goal that could not be achieved quickly, because the psychic and moral wounds were deep.

When there is talk of the year 1945, I am irritated by the phrase, 'the joy of victory'. What joy? So many people perished! Millions of bodies were buried! Thousands lost arms and legs. Lost sight and hearing. Lost their minds. Yes, we survived, but at what a cost! War is proof that man as a thinking and sentient being has failed, disappointed himself, and suffered defeat.

When there is talk of 1945, I remember that in the summer of that year my aunt, who miraculously made it through the Warsaw Uprising, brought her son, Andrzej, to visit us in the countryside. He was born during the uprising. Today he is a man in late middle-age,

254

and when I look at him I think how long ago it all was! Since then, generations have been born in Europe who know nothing of what war is. And yet those who lived through it should bear witness. Bear witness in the name of those who fell next to them, and often on top of them; bear witness to the camps, to the extermination of the Jews, to the destruction of Warsaw and of Wroclaw. Is this easy? No. We who went through the war know how difficult it is to convey the truth about it to those for whom that experience is, happily, unfamiliar. We know how language fails us, how often we feel helpless, how the experience is, finally, incommunicable.

And yet, despite these difficulties and limitations, we should speak. Because speaking about all this does not divide, but rather unites us, allows us to establish threads of understanding and community. The dead admonish us. They bequeathed something important to us and now we must act responsibly. To the degree to which we are able, we should oppose everything that could again give rise to war, to crime, to catastrophe. Because we who lived through the war know how it begins, where it comes from. We know that it does not begin only with bombs and rockets, but with fanaticism and pride, stupidity and contempt, ignorance and hatred. It feeds on all that, grows on that and from that. That is why, just as some of us fight the pollution of the air, we should fight the polluting of human affairs by ignorance and hatred. □

NOTES ON CONTRIBUTORS

Chimamanda Ngozi Adichie's first novel, *Purple Hibiscus*, is published by Fourth Estate in the UK and by Algonquin in the US. She is working on a second novel set in 1960s Nigeria.

Richard Beard is the author of four novels including *Damascus* (Vintage/Arcade) and *Dry Bones* (Vintage), and one book of non-fiction, *Muddied Oafs: The Last Days of Rugger* (Yellow Jersey).

Steve Featherstone is a writer and photographer. He lives in upstate New York.

Rodrigo Fresán was born in Argentina and now lives in Barcelona. His most recent novel, *Jardines de Kensington* (Mondadori), from which 'Never Neverland' is taken, will be published as *Kensington Gardens* by Faber in the UK and by Farrar, Straus & Giroux in the US.

Alexandra Fuller is the author of *Don't Let's Go to the Dogs Tonight* (Picador/Random House) and *Scribbling the Cat* (Picador/Penguin Press). She grew up in south-central Africa and now lives in Wyoming.

Masha Gessen's memoir, *Two Babushkas*, is published by Bloomsbury in the UK and Dial Press in the US as *Ester and Ruzya: How My Grandmothers Survived Hitler's War and Stalin's Peace*. She lives in Moscow.

Ryszard Kapuscinski was born in Poland in 1932. His books include *The Soccer War* and *Imperium* (Granta Books/Knopf). His most recent book, *Travels with Herodotus*, will be published by Allen Lane in the UK in 2006 and by Knopf in the US.

Jim Lewis's most recent novel is *The King is Dead* (Flamingo/Vintage).

Paul Maliszewski's writing has appeared in *Harper's*, *The Paris Review*, and *The Pushcart Prize* anthologies.

Ian McEwan's novel *Amsterdam* (Vintage/Anchor) won the Booker Prize in 1998. 'Lily' is taken from his new novel, *Saturday*, which will be published by Jonathan Cape in the UK and Nan A. Talese in the US in 2005.

John McGahern's novels include *The Barracks*, *The Dark* and *Amongst Women* (Faber/Penguin), which was shortlisted for the Booker Prize in 1990. An extract from his last novel, *That They May Face the Rising Sun* (Faber), was published in *Granta 75*. 'The Lanes' is taken from his forthcoming memoir which will be published by Faber in the UK and Knopf in the US.

Paul Theroux's most recent book is *The Stranger at the Palazzo D'Oro* (Hamish Hamilton/Houghton Mifflin). His new novel, *Blinding Light*, will be published by Hamish Hamilton. He is also a beekeeper in Hawaii.

Edmund White is the author of seventeen books. 'The Merry Widow' is taken from his just-completed memoir, *My Lives*, which will be published in 2005 by Bloomsbury in the UK and Ecco in the US. He teaches writing at Princeton.